PROLEGOMENA
FOR THE
OXFORD SHAKESPEARE

PROLEGOMENA
FOR THE
OXFORD SHAKESPEARE

A Study in Editorial Method

By

RONALD B. McKERROW

OXFORD
AT THE CLARENDON PRESS

Oxford University Press, Ely House, London W.1
GLASGOW NEW YORK TORONTO MELBOURNE WELLINGTON
CAPE TOWN SALISBURY IBADAN NAIROBI LUSAKA ADDIS ABABA
BOMBAY CALCUTTA MADRAS KARACHI LAHORE DACCA
KUALA LUMPUR SINGAPORE HONG KONG TOKYO

First published 1939
Reprinted lithographically in Great Britain
by Butler & Tanner Ltd
Frome and London
1969

PREFACE

WHEN in 1929 I began work upon this edition of the plays of Shakespeare in old spelling, I was far from realizing how little systematic consideration seemed ever to have been given to editorial methods as applied to English writings in general and those of Shakespeare in particular. Editors, while often very conscious of the imperfections in the work of their predecessors, appear for the most part to have regarded their task as the solution of a series of hardly related problems, each of which could be dealt with separately as it arose, and to have troubled themselves very little about laying down any general principles for their own guidance or securing any uniformity in the treatment of their author's writings as a whole.

Apart from a few pages contained in the preface to the older 'Cambridge' edition of 1863-6, and Professor Dover Wilson's 'Textual Introduction' to the 'New Cambridge Shakespeare' which appeared in the edition of *The Tempest* in 1921, there seems to be no connected discussion of the problems which confront the Shakespearian editor, for the question of emendation dealt with in Dr. Greg's valuable *Principles of Emendation in Shakespeare*, 1928, is, of course, only one part of the subject; and as in both cases the writers had in view the production of a modernized text, though these in their way were interesting and valuable I could derive little help from them. It was therefore necessary for me to construct for myself such a body of rules for editing as seemed both logical and workable. I had first to review the extant material upon which my texts must be based—for I regarded it as foreign to my purpose to discuss at any length the ancestry or provenance of that material or to theorize on the manuscripts or editions no longer extant. I had in particular to consider the criteria according to which the basic texts of my prints of the several plays should be selected; how closely the original texts should be followed both as regards the dialogue itself and its punctuation, and with respect to such accessories as act-division, stage directions, and speakers' names; what should be done as regards the variant readings of other editions than the one on which my text was based, and how such variants as I decided to record should be presented. Lastly, I had to consider the quantity and nature of the commentary, for it was my intention to give, in a concise and convenient form, not only all that could contribute to the establishment of the texts, but also whatever was necessary (and available) for their better understanding, while at the same time presenting all this secondary matter in such a way that it should be clearly subordinated to the text and should not distract the reader or spoil his pleasure in the plays themselves.

I began my task by working through the complete text of some ten plays, for it seems to me that it is only by actually doing the necessary editorial work up to the point at which it is ready for press that it is possible to test how one's *a priori* theories—for one must have theories of some kind on which to begin!—will work. To be quite frank, I found that much that had seemed to me sound and reasonable in the practice of former editors did not now stand the test of actual experience, and very little of my experimental work survived. As a result of these experiments I believe, however, that I have been able to devise methods of presenting both the texts and the accessory matter, which, if not in every respect completely logical, are at least practical and reasonably well fulfil the requirements which I had set before myself.

Of two things, at any rate, the preliminary work which I have done has convinced me. Firstly, that any satisfactory study of the works of Shakespeare, or indeed probably of any other author, must take full account of the order in which they were written, and that it is advisable actually to study them, so far as possible, in that order: and secondly that the adequate editing of a sixteenth- or seventeenth-century text is and must always remain a matter of experience and practice, as much as, or even more than, of theory. In particular I would protest against the view which seems now to be held by some, that the recovery of the texts of previous centuries is purely or even mainly a matter of bibliography or of linguistics, useful or even necessary as these 'sciences' are in their places, or that by methods of textual criticism we can ever arrive at certainty in the solution of our textual problems. Science is to-day so predominant in the affairs and actions of the world that a desire has grown up to bring within its scope, at least in name, many subjects which cannot properly be said to belong there, and *inter alia* to claim for textual criticism the qualities of a science and to refer to its methods as 'scientific'. Truth is truth and logic is logic, whether we are writing of the phenomena of gravitation or of the sources of a line of poetry, and in a sense any honestly conducted inquiry may be termed scientific; but the man of science, as science is usually understood, who builds up his theories on the basis of a series of propositions the truth of each of which can be demonstrated by experiments capable of repetition whenever desired, in circumstances which so far as their influence upon the results obtained is concerned are identical, is in a position to arrive at a very different order of certainty from the textual critic, to whom experiment is as a rule impossible. The latter can seldom, if ever, reproduce nowadays the conditions which influenced, or might have influenced, the transmission of the text with which he is concerned, and for scientific proof of his theories he must substitute arguments based on what seems to him, from his 'knowledge of human nature' and from what he can learn of the procedure and habits of early copyists, printers, and theatrical producers, most likely to have occurred, and which can seldom or never be more than *probably* correct, even though the probability may in some cases be of a high degree.

It might, indeed, be better if in the domain of literary research the words 'proof' and 'prove' were banished altogether from statements of results obtained, for they can seldom be appropriate even in the work of the youngest and least-experienced thesis-writer. Nothing can be gained, and much may be lost, by a pretence of deriving results of scientific accuracy from data which are admittedly uncertain and incomplete. In most cases all that we can show is that if the parties concerned in the transmission of a text behaved as we should expect them to have behaved, the copyist or compositor working with reasonable, but not excessive, attention to what was before him, the printer's reader bearing in mind, more or less constantly, that what he read was supposed to make such a partial kind of sense as could be looked for from poetry, and all other persons by whom the text could be affected behaving in a similarly normal manner, then such-and-such a theory of the history of the texts and their interrelationship is, on the evidence at present available, more probable than any suggested alternative.

Above all, let us remember that the thing most antipathetic to science is pseudo-science—far more indeed than informed and intelligent conjecture—a parade of the machinery of demonstration when such machinery is inappropriate, the amassing of statistics in cases where the phenomena are too diverse in character to be properly treated as units in an enumeration, the pretence that by bringing together arguments which individually are invalid one can arrive at proof, the elaborate listing of peculiarities of vocabulary, spellings, or what not which can be used to support a certain argument, while all which do not do so are silently ignored; in short, those attempts to compel belief by overwhelming the reader with a weight of evidence set out in a formal and ostensibly scientific manner and generally far too indigestible for assimilation, which, especially in the work of those researchers who seek after a degree rather than after truth, seem so often to take the place of that combination of knowledge and historical imagination which alone can help us to such *probable* reconstruction of events in the past as is as near as we can ever attain to scientific demonstration.

Let us, then, recognize that, important as it is, 'scientific' textual criticism has its very definite limitations. In association with philology it may be able to tell us with an approach to certainty what an author *might* have written or what, in view of his date, he *could not* have written; it can seldom give us much aid in guessing what he probably wrote. For this, or for such approach to a reasonable guess as is possible, we must depend mainly on such power as we may possess of understanding our author's mental habits, and indeed so far making them our own that, given the beginning of a train of thought, we may have some idea of its probable development and completion: and this is the affair not of science, but of an informed and disciplined imagination.

I am far from claiming to have any such qualifications myself, except perhaps such as one may automatically derive from a fairly wide reading in Elizabethan literature; and indeed it seems to me that much further research is still needed, especially of a linguistic nature, before any one can justly claim to have the knowledge and training necessary to acquire them. In two directions, however, excellent work is being done. On the one hand, year by year we learn more of the background of the Elizabethan period and of how the world of the sixteenth century appeared to Shakespeare and his contemporaries, as well as how he and they actually spoke and wrote; and on the other we are helped by special studies of the details of Shakespeare's individual style and imagery. Here again, however, we have need of textual criticism to prevent us from confusing the imagery which can safely be attributed to Shakespeare himself with what has been put into his mouth by his editors!

Indeed, when we sum up the whole matter, we shall, I think, find that the editing of an old text, however much it may call for literary appreciation and imagination, must in the first place be based upon the most careful research into surviving evidence, and that however much it may depend for its foundations upon that kind of common sense which some would dignify by the name of 'science', it is also, and perhaps in all its finer achievements, of the nature of an art.

May I close this preface with a few words of personal explanation and apology? When in 1910 I had finished my edition of the works of Thomas Nashe I conceived the ambitious project of an old-spelling Shakespeare edited with a much greater regard than was then customary to certain bibliographical considerations, the importance of which my work upon Nashe and other writers of his period had forced upon my notice. Just at that moment, however, another new edition of Shakespeare was announced which left no opening for my own project, and I therefore reluctantly put the matter from my mind. When, however, nearly twenty years later, to my great surprise, the Delegates of the Clarendon Press did me the honour to propose to me exactly the piece of work which I had been on the point of proposing to them in 1910, it seemed to me quite impossible to refuse their offer. Had I been wiser I should, no doubt, have realized that a man of my age, with only such time at his disposal as could be spared from the daily work by which he earned a living, had no business to think of undertaking a task of such magnitude as this, and I cannot help feeling that I owe some apology to those who may feel that my progress has been unduly slow. I trust, however, that what I have done in these last nine years may be found, when it is published, to have laid down lines on which good and useful work may proceed at a more reasonable pace.

The introduction which follows, which has grown gradually with the progress of the text upon which I was working, was in all essentials in its present shape by the autumn of 1937 and I was then in hopes that it would be published with the first two volumes (nine plays) of the edition in the course of this year (1938). A serious illness prevented me, however, from doing work of any kind from January last to September. In view of this interruption it has been decided that the introduction should be published at once, separately. It is hoped that the discussion of the methods of the edition, of which it mainly consists, will be of use to others engaged on textual work in the Shakespearian period.

It is a pleasure to record my indebtedness to my friend Dr. W. W. Greg, who very kindly read this introduction in its first form as long ago as 1933 or 1934, and with whom I have since discussed many of the matters of editorial practice with which it is concerned.

Finally, and especially, my hearty thanks are due to Dr. Alice Walker, who has been helping me in my Shakespearian work during the last three years, and whose acute and logical mind has in particular enabled me to straighten out very numerous details of method in connexion with the giving of collations, and who besides this has aided me enormously in what is perhaps the most difficult of an editor's tasks, namely, the securing of consistency in dealing with parallel problems in different plays. This requires constant reference back and forth in a large bulk of material—as well as an excellent memory—and without her help, I fear that it would have been impossible for me even to approach the uniformity of treatment which, between us, we have, I hope, achieved.

R. B. McK.

22 *December* 1938.

SUMMARY OF CONTENTS

THE PLAN OF THIS EDITION

THE PLAN OF THIS EDITION

THERE can be no edition of the work of a writer of former times which is satisfactory to all readers, though there might, I suppose, be at least half a dozen editions of the works of Shakespeare executed on quite different lines, each of which, to one group of readers, would be the best edition possible.[1] The great majority of those adults who now read Shakespeare may be presumed to do so on account of the pleasure which they obtain from his work as literature, old indeed, but dateless, and capable of imparting aesthetic satisfaction to persons of what we may call normal emotional experience quite without regard to its setting in time or place. For these, that edition is best which interposes the fewest possible obstacles between the modern reader without special training and his aesthetic appreciation of the text, niceties of verbal interpretation being matters of comparatively little moment. The 'best' text for such readers is likely to be one completely modernized both in spelling and punctuation, with full stage directions aiding them to visualize the action as it would be if staged by a reasonably conservative producer, and notes which explain as briefly as possible and without argument the commonly accepted meaning of unfamiliar words and difficult passages. At the other end of the scale are the comparatively few scholars, expert in the Elizabethan drama, whose interest lies mainly in textual minutiae or in bibliographical questions which may seem to have little or nothing to do with all that has made Shakespeare's work of value to the world. For these the 'best' edition will generally be a photographic reproduction of the early prints or, failing this, a facsimile reprint.

Between these two extremes come those editions which, with a greater or less degree of conservatism, attempt to present Shakespeare's work as nearly in the form in which he left it as the evidence which we have permits, clearing it indeed as far as possible of the numerous errors with which the ignorance and carelessness of copyists and printers have disfigured it, but without superfluous comment or any attempt to improve upon the text as the author left it. Of such

---

[1] Indeed, there can no more be a measure of the practical excellence of an edition apart from the persons by whom it is intended to be used, than there can be a measure of the aesthetic excellence of a work of art otherwise than in relation to the percipient mind.

editions, and among the more conservative of them, the present is intended to be one. The main purpose which I have kept before me throughout has been the establishment of the text, and for this it is believed that all available apparatus has been given. I have assumed in the reader a general knowledge of Elizabethan English, including the language of the Authorized Version of the Bible, but no special acquaintance with sixteenth-century grammar or phonology. I have assumed also an interest in textual questions and in the variant readings found in different editions so far, but in general[1] only so far, as these may conduce to the recovery or interpretation of the author's original wording. In the selection and presentation of these readings I have departed in many ways from the methods usually followed, and it is my hope that by so doing I have, while recording everything which can be of value to a reader or student of Shakespeare, succeeded in keeping my footnotes free from the accumulation of useless material which makes it difficult, in some of the most scholarly editions, to appreciate what is of real interest and value.

To me it seems that until recent times three principal causes have adversely affected the standard of Shakespearian editing. The first attempts to free his text from the numerous and evident corruptions of the early editions were made at a time when the only textual study was that of the classics, the problems of which were very different;[2] and it is doubtless due mainly to this fact that the critical methods employed by scholars in their work on Shakespeare and his contemporaries have been, and to some extent still are, ill thought-out and haphazard. Further, it is in one way unfortunate that, even now, the language of his time is not too remote from us for those whose acquaintance with English is limited to that of the present day to read him without difficulty, even if they do not always fully understand him. While no one would attempt to edit the work of Chaucer, or even of the later fifteenth-century writers, without at any rate some intensive study of the literature of their periods as a whole and a systematic attempt to ascertain the normal forms of the language in their author's time and locality, this seems seldom to have been regarded as a necessary preliminary to the editing of Shakespeare. Some, indeed, of his editors had read widely in the literature of his day and were able to cite numerous and most valuable parallels for the rarer words and phrases found in his works,

---

[1] See pp. 67–72, below.   [2] See p. 36, below.

as well as to explain many allusions to contemporary life and manners; but they troubled themselves, it would seem, little, if at all, about the everyday language of the period and often failed to interpret it correctly, or even, in some cases, to recognize it when they saw it. Lastly, the general practice of the earlier editors, with the exception of Capell, and of many of their modern successors, of working upon a recent edition in order to prepare their own, revising this when, and only when, it seemed to them in error, has tended to obscure the practices of the early texts and to give permanence to innumerable departures from them in points of detail.

More editorial labour has probably been expended on the writings of the Elizabethan and Jacobean periods than on any other portion of our literature, and yet there is no recent period of the language of which we have so little precise knowledge. The philologists have, until quite recently, concerned themselves hardly at all with anything after 1500. Old-spelling concordances or indexes are very few—there is not even one of Shakespeare himself—and such glossarial comment as exists is devoted almost entirely to uncommon words. The work of many of the more important dramatists and prose-writers of the time is still, in spite of much that has been done in recent years, only to be obtained in modernized editions,[1] and even work professing to deal with Shakespearian grammar has in some cases been based on editions of this kind in which the grammar has been emended in accordance with the views of modern editors.

In spite, therefore, of the immense amount that has been written about Shakespeare, one who should try to reconstruct an evidently corrupt passage of his text as he, or one of his contemporaries, might have written it may well, for lack of the necessary guidance, find his task a difficult or indeed impossible one.[2] We have now, of course, the great *Oxford English Dictionary*, which puts us in a far better position than his earlier editors as regards actual vocabulary, but

---

[1] Modernized at any rate as regards punctuation, even where the spelling of the early editions has been retained.

[2] It is, I think, the common experience of those who attempt the minuter study of Elizabethan authors to find, among the emendations of editors, phrases which strike them at once as 'not Elizabethan', while at the same time they are quite unable to say on what grounds such an opinion is based or to suggest an alternative expression which seems to them satisfactory or even 'possible'. It is, of course, a defect of our study of the language of Shakespeare's time that it is entirely one-sided. We should not expect to attain a real knowledge of French by merely reading it —however much we read—without at least some attempt to write or speak the language ourselves!

even this gives us only a small part of the information that we need as to the forms, constructions, and current meanings of the words which formed his language, and, of course, affords us no help at all concerning punctuation and such minor points of orthographical practice as word-division, hyphens, and apostrophes.

At the risk, therefore, of saying much that is, or should be, obvious, I feel that it is necessary to discuss in some detail what it is possible to do towards recovering the actual text of Shakespeare's writings and what I have attempted to do in this edition. I propose first to discuss the formation of the text itself, which, it will be seen, generally involves the choice of one of the early editions and the reproduction of this save where it appears to be wrong; secondly, the exactitude with which it is desirable to follow the chosen edition and the value of other editions than the one selected in supporting or amending the readings of this. Thirdly will come an explanation of the system adopted in presenting such readings of other editions as I have thought it desirable to record.

Before, however, we consider in detail the methods which have been here followed in attempting to reconstruct Shakespeare's text, a few words must be said as regards certain other matters of a general kind.

Firstly, as regards the scope of the edition, it is proposed to include all the plays which are generally attributed either wholly or in part to Shakespeare.[1] These will be printed in as close an approximation as is possible to the order in which they were composed. The actual order cannot of course be exactly ascertained, as the dates of a few plays are still in dispute, and in any case there are certain ones which may have been completed or revised some years after they were first taken in hand and to which therefore no single date can be assigned. There is, however, I think, very general agreement among scholars that the dates assigned to the plays in Sir Edmund Chambers's *William Shakespeare*, i. 270–1, are at any rate approximately correct, and I shall therefore follow the order there given with only such slight modification as is necessary to bring the three parts of *Henry VI* into their customary order,[2] together with a few other minor adjustments intended to render the volumes of more equal size. The poems will be

---

[1] Whether or not certain doubtful plays in which some believe Shakespeare had a hand, such as *Sir Thomas More*, *Edward III*, and *The Two Noble Kinsmen*, are to be included is reserved for future consideration.

[2] Chambers assigns to Part I the date 1591–2 and to Parts II and III, 1590–1. It

printed, as is usual, at the end of the edition, together, it is hoped, with those Quartos (the generally called 'bad' Quartos) which present a text differing too greatly from that generally accepted for it to be possible to give their readings conveniently in footnotes.

Other features of the edition such as the collation notes, the introductions to the several plays, and the explanatory notes are sufficiently discussed below.

is probably true that the plays were written in this order, but as Part I, *in its present form*, is clearly intended to precede Part II, it would be very awkward to print it as the last of the trilogy.

I
THE BASIS OF A REPRINT

FOR scholarly purposes, the ideal text of the works of an early dramatist would be one which, on the positive side, should approach as closely as the extant material allows to a fair copy, made by the author himself, of his plays in the form which he intended finally to give them, and, on the negative side, should not in any way be coloured by the preconceived ideas or interpretations of later times.

That, indeed, may be said to be the ideal, but it must be admitted that, in the case of Shakespeare at any rate, it is and is likely always to remain a very distant one. In the first place it is very doubtful whether, especially in the case of the earlier plays, there ever existed any written 'final form'. Shakespeare as an active member of a theatrical company would, at any rate in his younger days, have been concerned with producing, not plays for the study, but material for his company to perform on the stage, and there can be little doubt that his lines would be subject to modification in the light of actual performance, as well as to later revision when, for example, a change in the constitution of the company necessitated a redistribution of the roles, or a desire was felt to introduce some topical allusion or to parody or improve upon some rival show.[1] Such alterations may have been made by the author himself or, if he was not available, they may have been made by others. He may, or may not, have regarded them as improvements: he probably merely accepted them as necessary changes, and it is quite likely that he never bothered about whether they introduced inconsistencies into what was originally conceived as a consistent whole. We must not expect to find a definitive text in the sense in which the published version of the plays of a modern dramatist is definitive.

And even in those plays which do seem to us to be finished wholes, written at one time with a single impulse of the creative spirit, and which show no signs of tampering or revision whether by the original

---

[1] In particular, less important characters were liable to be cut out or fused into one, as in the case of Ratcliff and Lovel in *Richard III* and probably Southwell in *2 Henry VI*; see too Chambers, *Shakespeare*, i. 121, n. 1. It is also clear that the number of minor characters was often left undetermined, as is shown by such directions as '*Enter three or foure*', *C. of E.*, IV. iv. 100, or '*others as many as can be*', *Tit. And.*, I. i. 72.

author or by another, we cannot be certain of any close approach to the author's manuscript. Seeing that, with the exception of one possible fragment, we have neither any autograph manuscript of Shakespeare, nor even any manuscript copy of such a manuscript,[1] and are compelled to rely, for any idea that we can form of a Shakespearian original, on printed texts of uncertain but undoubtedly varied provenance, we cannot hope to infer with any approach to certainty Shakespeare's own practice as regards such details as spelling, capitalization, the use of italics, or punctuation. As, therefore, we cannot deduce rules for normalization, the only possible course is to determine for each play separately the most authoritative text of those which have come down to us from early times, and to reprint this as exactly as possible save for manifest and indubitable errors. Such a method will no doubt give us a series of texts which are less uniform in the details of presentation than those to which we are accustomed in modern-spelling editions, but this cannot be helped. The alternative of normalization on an insufficient basis would be very much worse.

Our first task in the case of each play will then be to determine the most authoritative text, the one which, on the evidence available, we must suppose to come nearest to what Shakespeare wrote, and for this purpose we must of course take into account the history and interrelationship of the early printed editions.

Now the 'most authoritative text' is evidently not necessarily that one of the extant texts which is earliest in its date of printing, for such earliest print may, of course, have been derived from a more corrupt source than some other later one. Nor is it necessarily the most 'correct' text, i.e. that which contains the greatest number of readings which probably correspond to those of the author's manuscript, for it is to be hoped that the modern editions of Shakespeare come closer to his manuscript in wording, if not in spelling, than any of the sixteenth- or seventeenth-century editions. Indeed, if they do not, the labours of editors have been in vain! The 'most authoritative' text is, at least for our present purpose, something different. It is that one of the early[2] texts which, on a consideration

---

[1] The few manuscripts of Shakespeare's plays, or of portions of them, which have come down to us appear all to be copies from printed books and without textual value. They include forty-two lines of *Titus Andronicus*, parts of *1, 2 Henry IV*, and presumably the whole of *Twelfth Night* and the *Merry Wives* (see Chambers, *Shakespeare*, i. 313, 378, 404, 425).

[2] 'Early' is a vague term, but as applied to editions of Shakespeare it is generally

of their genetic relationship, appears likely to have deviated to the smallest extent in all respects of wording, spelling, and punctuation from the author's manuscript.

Consideration of the various early texts which have come down to us will show us, as a rule without any doubt, that in the case of any play there is at least one edition, and in the case of some plays more than one, which cannot have been derived from any other edition now extant, the source of such edition or editions having presumably been either a manuscript or an edition which has perished; and that others of these texts, i.e. in most cases all those which bear the later dates, are derived,[1] with or without intentional modification, from earlier extant editions. Let us call the texts of the first group 'substantive' texts;[2] those of the second 'derived' texts. It is evident that the 'most authoritative text' of which we are in search must be a 'substantive' one.

It is, of course, obvious that these substantive printed texts, through which has descended to us whatever knowledge we possess of our author's original manuscript, may stand in a variety of different relations to that original manuscript. The compositor, when setting one of them up, may have had the original manuscript before him, in which case, if the manuscript had been finally revised and tidied up by the author, the printer should have been able to produce an almost perfect text;[3] in the case of another, he may have had only a copy at second or third hand, or perhaps one altered for the purposes of the theatre; for a third, he may have had no more than a manuscript botched together by some one who had taken down, by shorthand or some other method, the gist of a performance which he had witnessed on the stage; for a fourth, a copy of a printed edition the whole of which has now perished, and so on; the possibilities are, as is well known, very numerous.

The general character of the copy from which the substantive text (or texts) of a work was set up can often be determined with

taken to include all the editions of the separate plays issued before the First Folio of 1623, together with that Folio itself.

[1] Not, of course, necessarily *immediately* derived, for there may be intermediate editions now lost.

[2] I am not aware that 'substantive' has been used previously in the sense which I am here attributing to it, but it is defined (*O.E.D.*) as 'having an independent existence or status; not dependent upon, subsidiary to, or referable to something else'. We have, of course, for our present purpose, to understand the word 'extant' after 'else'.

[3] At any rate verbally, though he would not necessarily follow what he looked upon as the author's eccentricities as regards spelling, &c.

some degree of probability,[1] and when this is possible it is of concern to an editor, as it naturally has a bearing on the degree of credence which he should give to the readings of the substantive texts in question. I have therefore discussed the general character of the various texts in the appropriate introductions.

In recent years, however, such investigations have become increasingly far-reaching, and attempts have been made to explain the manifest or presumed defects in Shakespearian texts by means of theories often involving the assumption of an extremely complicated history.[2] We are asked to suppose the incorporation of parts of lost plays, revision by several different hands for different theatrical or other purposes, that the text was copied by one person, the stage directions by another, and so on, until we sometimes feel that while the theory would no doubt explain well enough the disturbances to which the text appears to have been subjected, it would equally well serve to explain a far greater amount of disturbance than seems actually to have occurred.

These investigations have frequently been ingenious and even brilliant, and they are of undoubted value provided that we recognize their limitations and realize that the greater part of the conclusions reached are, and must always remain, guess-work. If we find a text containing, say, certain errors or inconsistencies which we feel convinced that no intelligent author could have deliberately intended to stand, we shall as a rule find that such errors may be explained in a number of very different ways and that there is no criterion by which we can ascertain which explanation is correct. To mention a few of the more obvious possibilities, there may have been mere carelessness or indifference on the part of the author, who may have been handing over his manuscript sheet by sheet to the theatre as he wrote and have never bothered about any final revision, trusting to put right

---

[1] For example, I have attempted to show that a certain kind of variation in the speakers' names indicates derivation from the author's original manuscript, rather than from a fair copy prepared by a theatrical copyist. See *R.E.S.*, xi (1935), 459–65. At the foot of p. 463 *King John* should be deleted and it should be noted that in the case of the *Taming of the Shrew* only the play itself is meant, not the Induction.

[2] It is, I think, very unfortunate that attempts to determine the causes of the condition of the texts seem to have come to be called by the general name of 'bibliographical' study of these texts. The only reason for the name seems to be that some of the principal scholars who have interested themselves in such research, such as Dr. A. W. Pollard and Dr. W. W. Greg, have *also* been bibliographers. There is nothing particularly 'bibliographical' about most of the arguments used.

any too glaring inconsistencies at the time of the rehearsal; the play may have been revised on one or more occasions and the manuscript which was used for printing may have represented some kind of incomplete revision; or an imperfect manuscript may have been the only one available to the printer and this may have been completed by guess-work. As a rule there is no means of determining what actually did happen. The most that we can do is select the explanation which, in view of what we know or guess as to the processes through which the manuscript seems likely to have passed or the accidents to which it seems likely to have been subjected, appears the *simplest*. But, even so, what right have we to suppose that the simplest explanation of a fact is necessarily the true one? Sometimes indeed there might even be a simpler explanation than any of those which are usually put forward, namely, that author, printers, and all concerned were at times all drunk together, as indeed some of the earlier editors seem to have supposed when they desired to rid themselves of any responsibility for too close following of the old texts! But such an explanation would nowadays be regarded as *too* simple. We seek for something which, while not involving so drastic a cutting of the Gordian knot, will explain the obviously unsatisfactory condition of the texts in a way which will strike the reader as ingenious without putting too great a strain on his credulity.

It has not seemed to me worth while to discuss at any considerable length the possible history of the copy used in printing any of the extant 'substantive' texts of Shakespeare. I have in each case briefly summarized any views which I know to be held by those scholars who have given attention to the matter, but as a rule the arguments in favour of their views cannot be fairly presented except at very great length, while even more space would be required by an attempt to refute them. As I have said, it seems to me in most cases impossible to arrive at any certainty—or even at any reasonable probability—in such matters, and I have therefore made no attempt to argue them.

We must then first determine which of the extant texts are what I have called 'substantive' editions, i.e. not derived as a whole, or to any considerable extent,[1] from another extant edition, and which are derived editions; and having done this we must ascertain how each of the derived texts is related to the substantive edition from which

---

[1] We must, of course, consider the general mass of the text. It is quite possible that an edition which is 'substantive' in that ninety-nine hundredths of it are based

it is immediately or ultimately descended, and how it is related to other derived texts of the same group.[1] As a result of this examination we shall, as a rule, be able to exhibit our texts in groupings such as the following:

(*a*) One substantive text, three derived.

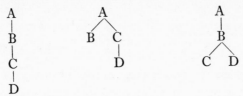

(*b*) Two substantive texts, three derived.

Now let us consider the results from the point of view of textual criticism of these two different arrangements. In the case of (*a*), where all the texts go back to a single extant text, provided the copy for the derived texts was not corrected by Shakespeare himself or by direct reference to his manuscript it is evident that every reading in the later editions, B, C, and D, other than additional matter, misprints, and conjectural emendations, must be derived from A and therefore that *no reading of B, C, or D which differs from the corresponding reading of A can possibly have any authority whatsoever*. There is

on a source of which no earlier derivative is extant, may yet contain passages which are derived from another extant edition. A case of this kind is that of *2, 3 Henry VI*, where the Folio text was as a whole evidently printed from a manuscript, but nevertheless contains a few passages derived from the *Contention* and the *True Tragedy*, the obvious explanation being that the manuscript was in places defective, and the editor or compositor did his best to complete the play from these earlier Quartos; see my 'Note on the "Bad Quartos" of *2, 3 Henry VI*' in *R.E.S.*, xiii (1937), 64–72. We must call such a text 'substantive' in spite of these passages of reprinted matter.

On the other hand, new readings, either misprints or intentional corrections, which occur in what is as a whole a 'derived' text cannot make the edition in which they appear a 'substantive' one. Nor should we regard a text as substantive on the ground of its containing an additional passage or scene (such as the 'deposition scene' of *Richard II* or the 'fly' scene of *Titus Andronicus*), except of course in so far as concerned the passage or scene in question.

[1] For some discussion as to the methods by which the interrelationship of printed editions can generally be determined, see Appendix B. There are, as a rule, much simpler and quicker ways of determining this than by a full comparison of readings.

no question of B or C being of secondary or 'middle' authority as some of the earlier editors phrased it. These texts can have no *Shakespearian* authority whatever and, though these editions may be of use to us in the subsidiary way mentioned on pp. 37–8, below, a reading introduced into a modern text from any one of them will be as much a 'conjectural' reading as one which is entirely the modern editor's own invention. It is therefore obvious that when we find editions grouping themselves in this way the earliest must necessarily be taken as the copy-text.[1]

It is important to observe that once a text has deviated in any respect from its copy, no restoration of the original readings by guess-work, however convincing or indeed 'certain' we may regard it, can in any way cancel that deviation or become 'authoritative' in the sense in which we are using the word. Thus, for example, in *The Comedy of Errors*, I. ii. 65–7,

> For she will scoure your fault vpon my pate:
> Me thinkes your maw, like mine, should be your cooke,
> And strike you home without a messenger . . .

the accepted readings in modern spelling are 'score' for 'scoure' and 'clock' for 'cooke', these being respectively the emendations of Rowe and Pope. There can be little or no doubt that these readings are what was originally intended by the author, but however certain we may feel of this, the only readings which have any *authority* are 'scoure' and 'cooke'. Those which have been admitted into the usual text are merely conjectural emendations to be ranked with any other guesses.

I shall use then 'authoritative reading' for any reading which may be presumed to derive by direct descent from the manuscript of the author. Thus all readings in whatever text appears to stand in the closest relation of all extant texts to the author's manuscript will be termed 'authoritative', with the exception of such readings as are on the face of them miscopyings or misprints. In a sense, even these are authoritative, or at least we may say that they have more authority than the corrections of later editions, even when we may feel that we can accept such corrections as restoring what must have stood in the author's manuscript. It would, however, be rather absurd to term simple and obvious misprints in an earliest edition 'authoritative'

---

[1] I use this term, 'copy-text', first employed, I believe, in the 'Note on the Treatment of the Text' in my edition of *The Works of Thomas Nashe*, vol. i, 1904, p. xi, to mean 'the text used in each particular case as the basis of mine'.

when we know that it is much more likely that they are due to the printer of the edition than to the manuscript from which he worked, and that they would certainly have been rejected by the author if they had come under his notice.

When, however, we have such an arrangement of the texts as is described under (*b*), namely, when the later ones do not all go back to a single extant edition, the case is quite otherwise. Any one of the texts which stands at the head of an extant series or which is independent of the others *may* be the one which represents most accurately the author's manuscript, and it is only by consideration of the readings themselves and by the use of our own judgement that we can decide which edition should be used as copy-text. Fortunately, in many cases one is so much inferior to the other or others, as in the case of the 'bad' Quartos, that there can be little doubt, but in others such as *Hamlet* Q2 and F1, *Lear*, and *Othello* problems of great difficulty and complexity arise. It is obvious that what has been said on pages 11 and 12 concerning the want of authority in derived texts will apply equally well, *mutatis mutandis*, to the derived texts of this grouping, i.e. C, D, and E in the first example, B, D, and E in the second.

It would, I think, be convenient if we could use some such words as 'monogenous' and 'polygenous' to designate the two groupings of texts which I have described above: 'monogenous' standing for those which derive from a single extant edition and 'polygenous' for those which have at their head two or more extant editions none of which derives from another—substantive texts, as I have called them above (p. 8). The difference is a fundamental one in all textual criticism, though for several reasons of less practical application in the case of manuscripts than of printed books, and the neglect to observe it has led to much editorial confusion.

For example, critics have frequently insisted that the 'best' or 'most correct' of the early texts should be selected as the basis of a new edition, but it does not seem always to have been appreciated that it is only when the choice is between two substantive texts that correctness, in the sense of freedom from obvious errors, can be taken as a criterion in this selection. Obviously, if a work has been transmitted to us in several manuscripts or printed editions, none of which appears to have been copied or printed from another, and all of which may have originated during the lifetime of the author, it will, in the absence of any external evidence as to the relationship of the texts, be the duty of an editor to select for the basis of a new edition that text which in his judgement is most representative of the author and most nearly in accord with what, in view of his other works, we should have expected from him at the date to which the work in question is assigned. In the majority of cases this will mean simply that the editor must select the text which appeals most to his critical judgement, and this, in its turn, will as a rule be the one which appears to be the most careful copy of its original and the most free from obvious errors.

It is, however, quite a different matter when there is question of a choice among texts of which the later are clearly derived[1] from a single early one which we possess. In such a case one of the later texts may be markedly superior in general 'correctness' to the others. It may be freer from misprints and from grammatical errors or peculiarities, much smoother in rhythm, and defective lines in the earlier editions may have been made good: it may, in short, have been carefully edited for the press. This, however, would not in itself be the smallest reason for taking it as the basis of a new edition, for our aim is of course not merely to produce a text free from irregularities— if it were this, we might take the Cambridge text as a basis—but one as near as possible to what the author wrote.[2] All depends on the identity of the corrector and on his authority for making the corrections. If we had external evidence that a particular text of any work had been revised throughout *by its author*, such a text should undoubtedly be made the basis of a modern edition,[3] but such cases are rare and, so far as I am aware, it has never been suggested that there is such external evidence of correction in the case of any Shakespearian play. In the great majority of instances of 'correction'[4] in later editions

---

[1] When we say that a text is derived from another, we of course only mean that the latter has been the *main* source for it; any *variants* which it contains are obviously not derived from that source. In so far as these are concerned we have a case of different sources even though one of these may be merely the imagination of the corrector!

[2] Two things are necessary for the production of a good edition of a text: (1) an authoritative text on which to base the reproduction, and (2) conscientious care on the part of the producer. In the case of the Shakespearian texts we find that, as a rule, the two requirements are, so to say, crossed. The first printer of the text (other than a bad Quarto) had the most authoritative text to work from, but on the other hand he seems sometimes to have been the least careful and conscientious of all who have ever tried to put the text in print.

[3] Unless, of course, we wish to present the work in what is admittedly an early form.

[4] By 'correction' I mean the presence of such changes as can hardly be accidental or due to the printer's inadvertence.

we have no external evidence whatever as to the source of the changes, and are therefore compelled to consider whether in themselves they show any signs of being made by the author of the work, or, on the other hand, are such as might be due to a corrector of the press or editor; for in the latter case we must of course ignore them completely in considering whether we should make the text in which they appear the basis of our modern edition. This has nothing to do with the merit or demerit of the corrections in themselves, for some at least may almost certainly represent what the author wrote and we may reasonably adopt them in our text,[1] but it does mean that when we have to consider whether the superior 'correctness' of a later text entitles it to be used as the basis of a modern edition, we must begin by eliminating as of no evidential value all such corrections as might easily be made by another than the author.

Thus no attention whatever should, in this connexion, be paid to such as the following:

1. Correction or normalization of spelling, punctuation, or grammar.

2. Corrections of metre resulting in the supplying of syllables necessary for the smoothing of rhythm or in the removal of those which are metrically superfluous. For example, in the line

> What is thy sentence but speechlesse death?
> (*Rich. II*, 1. iii. 172. Q1–5)[2]

the First Folio inserts 'then' after 'sentence' and thus makes the line metrically regular. It seems quite possible that 'then' is correct, but the insertion is obviously well within the powers of any proof-reader of average intelligence and there is no reason whatever to see the author's hand in it. Some critics have written as if the improvement of 'rough' metre were a proof of the use of the author's manuscript, but as a matter of fact such 'improvement' is the easiest of all forms of revision for any person with a normal appreciation of rhythm. Nor need we see the author's hand in the touching-up of prose lines so as to render them metrical, which is almost equally simple.

3. Any such corrections as can easily be made by reference to the

---

[1] If edition A misprints the word 'heauen' as 'heanen' and B has it correct, we shall naturally accept the correction, but such a correction or a thousand similar ones have not the slightest bearing on the question whether A or B is the 'best' text on which to base a reprint.

[2] Throughout this introduction, references are to my forthcoming edition. Though the line numbering will not always tally with that of standard editions, the reader should have no difficulty in finding the line or passage referred to.

immediate context, as for example when a letter is quoted twice with different wording and the two quotations are brought into accord in a later edition. Obviously the later edition is 'corrected', but equally obviously, as the correction could have been made by any person capable of reading, there is no need to attribute it to the author or to suppose that the proof-reader compared the text with a manuscript. Indeed, I think that it might fairly be argued that when a work of imagination is so revised as to produce mechanical correctness in minor matters which do not affect its dramatic or poetical quality, while at the same time it contains no alterations which do affect these, we may assume with some confidence that the author had no hand in the revision.[1]

It is, then, only after we have eliminated all such corrections as can with probability be attributed to an editor that we can begin to consider whether such changes as remain are likely to have any real authority, and here we may be faced by the most difficult problems which textual criticism has to offer. We shall, however, I think, find that in the majority of cases where a derived text shows what seem to be intentional variants from, or corrections of, its immediate predecessor, all these changes are such as might have been, and commonly were, made by correctors of the press, and that there is no reason to assume the use of any source (save the 'corrector's' imagination) other than the text from which it was printed.

While, however, it is very seldom indeed that we come across alterations which suggest more than the hand of a rather careless proof-corrector, it must be admitted that there are several ways in which variant readings in a later member of a series *may* be genuine.

(*a*) It is possible that an author may himself have corrected a copy of a particular edition, and that this corrected copy may have been used as copy-text for a subsequent edition. This is, of course, the common method which has, I suppose at all times, been used by authors who wished mistakes which they found in their works to be put right in subsequent editions; the result being that while a particular edition has evidently been printed from the preceding one and has taken over many of its errors and introduced others of its own, here and there it has a good new reading.[2] It is obvious that the author's

---

[1] As every publisher knows, it is seldom that a present-day author can correct his work in formal details without wishing at the same time to amend it in more important matters.

[2] A slightly different case of this may be found in the eighth edition of Gray's *Elegy*, 1753, which claims to have been 'Corrected by the Author' and which, while

corrected copy might survive the author himself and that by this means genuine readings might first appear in an edition printed long after his death.

(*b*) It is possible that, in the case of plays such as Shakespeare's, the company with which he was associated may have had manuscripts of his, even of those plays which for the First Folio were set up from Quartos, and the Quartos used may have been corrected to a greater or less extent from such manuscripts. This has, for example, been held to be the case with part of the Folio text of *Richard II*.[1]

(*c*) It is supposed that some of the Quartos used as copy for F1 had been used in the theatre as prompt-copies. It is possible that these contained corrections, either made by Shakespeare, in which case they may have been improvements subsequent to the original writing of the play, or derived from actors or other members of the company who were familiar with the play as acted.

These are, I think, the principal ways in which we might expect authentic corrections of reading to appear in texts which are printed in the main from an earlier edition, though there are, no doubt, other possibilities. These, however, should be enough to make it clear that even when the extant early texts consist of a series each of which served as copy for the printer of the next, we cannot exclude the possibility that certain readings only found in the later editions may be authentic. Unfortunately, however, in the great majority of cases, there is no means of deciding whether they are authentic or not, and though there may be a few readings of which we can say with some approach to certainty that they are *not* Shakespeare's, there are few, if any, of which we can safely make the opposite assertion.

Even if, however, we were to assure ourselves on what seemed quite satisfactory evidence that certain corrections found in a later edition of a play were of Shakespearian authority, it would not by any means follow that that edition should be used as the copy-text of a reprint. It would undoubtedly be necessary to incorporate these corrections in our text, but unless we could show that the edition in question (or the copy from which it had been printed) had been

including a number of new readings, contains an error which Gray had pointed out previously and which had been corrected in at least one edition, suggesting that the printer had had the use of a copy corrected by Gray and had simply transferred the corrections from this to the less correct edition from which he was printing (see *R.E.S.*, vii (1931), 108).

[1] Cambridge edition, 1863–6, vol. iv, p. ix.

gone over and corrected throughout by Shakespeare, a thing in the highest degree unlikely, it seems evident that, allowing for the usual continuous degeneration customary in reprinted texts, this later edition will (except for the corrections) deviate more widely than the earliest print from the author's original manuscript. This deviation is likely to be mainly apparent in spelling and punctuation, neither of which would matter if the text were to be used as the basis of a modern-spelling edition, as both would be normalized, but which matter greatly in the case of an edition of the type of the present one. We may indeed, I think, take it as certain that in all ordinary circumstances the nearest approach to our ideal of an author's fair copy of his work in its final state will be produced by using the earliest 'good' print as copy-text and inserting into it, from the first edition which contains them, such corrections as appear to us to be derived from the author.

At first sight this may appear likely to give a very similar result to the eclectic method of Pope, who took from the various Quartos any readings which pleased him and inserted them into his text, apparently considering that whatever pleased him was good and that whatever was good must be Shakespeare's: but there is really a world of difference in the two methods. We are not to regard the 'goodness' of a reading in and by itself, or to consider whether it appeals to our aesthetic sensibilities or not; we are to consider whether a particular edition taken *as a whole* contains variants from the edition from which it was otherwise printed which could not reasonably be attributed to an ordinary press-corrector, but by reason of their style, point, and what we may call inner harmony with the spirit of the play as a whole, seem likely to be the work of the author: and once having decided this to our satisfaction we must accept *all* the alterations of that edition, saving any which seem obvious blunders or misprints.

It may be said at once that in the case of those plays of which the First Folio gives us the earliest text, no question of the selection of a copy-text or of the author's corrections arises, for there is no reason to attach any authority to the readings of any later text. When, however, there is an earlier Quarto edition it will be necessary in each particular case to consider the relation of later Quartos, if any, and of the First Folio to it, and to attempt to determine whether the variant readings of any of these later editions can have any authority. This attempt will be made in the introductions to the several plays.

II

THE DEGREE OF EXACTITUDE TO BE AIMED AT IN REPRODUCING THE COPY-TEXT

HAVING, then, in the case of each play selected from among the early editions the one which is to be used as the basis of the text to be printed here, which will as a general rule be the earliest edition except in cases where such edition presents the text in a manifestly imperfect or corrupt form, we must next consider the degree of exactitude which is to be aimed at in reproducing this early text. It is evident that a facsimile reprint of the original with all its errors is, in an edition of the present kind, neither possible nor desirable, and that something between this and a normalized edition, which for reasons already given is impossible, must be attempted. It will be necessary to discuss in some detail the method which has been adopted.

But we must, I think, at the outset distinguish between the actual text of the plays, in the sense of the matter which is intended to be spoken by the characters, and such accessories as act and scene headings, the speakers' names, and to some extent also the stage directions, for so far at least as the *form* of these accessories is concerned there is clear evidence that in some cases this was due to the printers. Thus the Latin heading '*Actus primus, Scena prima*', which occurs in one spelling or another at the head of every play in the First Folio save three, was, as has been clearly shown, often made to serve for several plays without resetting—one setting being used, as the broken letters show, in no less than twenty out of the thirty-six plays.[1] It is evident, then, that the form of this at least was not derived from the author's manuscripts, but that the printers were alone responsible for it. Similarly the speakers' names evidently depend for their form, or at any rate for the extent to which they are abbreviated, on the amount of room that there is for them in the line.[2] Thus in *King*

[1] See E. E. Willoughby, *The Printing of the First Folio* (Supplement to the *Bibliographical Soc. Transactions*, No. 8, 1932), pp. 14–16.

[2] I am not referring here to the variation in the actual names given to the speakers in some plays, as where 'Gloucester' alternates with 'Humphrey', or 'Angelo' with 'Goldsmith'. This is a much more important matter and may, in my view, give us valuable indications of the relation of the copy used by the printer to the author's original manuscript. See pp. 9, n. 1, 56–7.

Lear the king's name as that of a speaker is normally given in full as '*Lear.*': when, however, the line happens to be a full one the name is abbreviated to '*Lea.*' or '*Le.*'. So in other plays we may find '*King.*' abbreviated when necessary to '*K.*', or '*Queene.*' given as '*Queen.*', '*Qu.*', or '*Q.*',[1] the shorter forms being always used when the line is exceptionally full, though occasionally elsewhere. As it cannot be supposed that a *writer* would vary the form according to the length of line which was to follow,[2] this variation must be attributed to the compositor. Both in the case of the act headings and of the speakers' names, it seems therefore the more reasonable course to adopt a uniform system throughout and to ignore the form of the original in particular cases.

We may thus distinguish between the text of the plays, which should be reproduced so far as possible without change, and accessories, in which normalization is allowable.[3] The methods followed in this normalization will be discussed later.

THE TEXT

As regards the text it has been my purpose to reproduce as exactly as possible, letter for letter, and point for point, what is given to us by the extant records, namely by those 'originals' which, considered as wholes, appear to transmit to us most accurately what we may suppose Shakespeare to have written; departing from them only where they appear to be certainly corrupt, as well as in certain purely typographical points enumerated below.[4]

[1] e.g. in *2 Henry VI.*

[2] There is no uniformity of practice in the extant manuscripts of plays, though perhaps the most frequent method was to write the names in full in stage directions and abbreviate them, sometimes to a single initial, in the speakers' names.

[3] It is not pretended that the typographical necessity of crowding the longer lines —especially in such a narrow measure as that of the First Folio—would not affect the spelling of the text itself, for often it has obviously done so. In this case, however, we have no norm to follow, whereas in that of the speakers' names we commonly have.

[4] The following are the principal exceptions to the rule of exact (typographical) reproduction. In deference to current (though, I think, wrong) opinion s is substituted for f. Further, w is printed for vv; wrong-fount letters and points are corrected; ornamental initials are replaced by plain ones and the capital letter which commonly followed an ornamental initial is replaced by a lower-case one. Running headlines, catchwords, and signatures, being outside the text-page, are normally omitted. For the treatment of act and scene headings, speakers' names, &c., see below, pp. 49–60. For the way in which turned, broken, and wrong-fount letters have been dealt with see Appendix A, as also for certain other minor departures from the practice of the original, such as the manner of presenting songs and inci-

But what is meant by 'certainly corrupt'? It may seem that the expression is clear enough, but it may in fact be extremely difficult to decide whether a word or phrase found in an early text is properly to be regarded as corrupt or not,[1] and some discussion of the point is necessary.

To begin with, we may regard as 'certainly corrupt' any form which, in the light of our knowledge of the language at the time when the text in question was written, was 'impossible', that is, would not have been, in its context, an intelligible word or phrase. Such a form may be either a simple misprint caused by the compositor's failure to set up what he intended or by some accident to the type after composition, or it may be an error of a more complicated kind caused by the compositor or some anterior copyist having failed to read or copy his original correctly.

A simple misprint is, as a rule, due to the accidental substitution of one letter for another, or the omission, addition, or transposition of one or more letters, e.g. the word 'cas' printed for 'has' or 'lonie' for 'onlie'. If a form found in the copy-text is of this kind and if it is certain from the context what word is intended,[2] it seems clearly the duty of an editor to substitute the correct word, though he will do well to indicate in a footnote exactly how the word stood in the copy-text. Many such simple misprints can, of course, be corrected at sight with almost complete certainty, and in fact they were generally corrected in the first reprint which was made of the text. At the same time, however, we find as a rule many things altered even in the earliest reprints which, whether or not they were errors in the originals, were evidently regarded as erroneous, or at least as unusual or antiquated forms,[3] at the time of the reprint. When we try to reproduce the original text it is often exceedingly difficult to determine whether such things as these should be regarded as having, so

dental verse, and of dealing with the abbreviated names which sometimes occur in the text.

[1] The development of Shakespearian editing since the time of Pope has largely consisted in restoring to the text words and expressions which he had rejected as corrupt.

[2] It is, of course, necessary that no other words equally near to the form found should fit the context, such as 'case' or 'was', 'lonlie' or 'honie'.

[3] It is to be remembered that until English became a subject of study *all* reprints of books of all classes were automatically modernized by being brought into accordance with the orthography and punctuation of their own day. The degree of modernization simply depended on the care with which the work was done.

to say, always been erroneous, or as having become erroneous by the lapse of time and change in language or orthography. Obviously we must distinguish very carefully between a correction of a real error in the original and a modernization or normalization, and not assume that a word or phrase is corrupt merely because it is altered in the first reprint which was made of the text in which it appears.

An example may make the point clearer. Suppose that in a certain original we find the word 'aloft' printed in one place 'a loft', though everywhere else it is 'aloft', the single 'a loft' being altered in the first reprint. Are we to regard this as a misprint and correct it to 'aloft', as we should certainly do if it had been misprinted 'al oft'? On the one hand we might argue that the fact that the word generally appears as 'aloft' is a sufficient indication that that was the spelling intended and that neither the author nor the compositor is at all likely to have purposely spelt it otherwise in one particular case; and that it is therefore merely a misprint and should be corrected. On the other hand, however, we must remember that in 'aloft' and a number of similar words we frequently at an earlier date, and occasionally even later, find the 'a' printed as a separate word,[1] and we might argue from this that the form cannot be counted as an error, but is merely a different spelling to be treated on the same footing as any other spelling which occurs occasionally. Moreover, the fact that 'a loft' occurs only once in the printed text which we are considering does not preclude the possibility of 'a loft' having been the regular spelling of the manuscript. The compositor may have intended to normalize this throughout to the more orthodox 'aloft', and then in a single instance failed to do so.

It is evidently not of any importance in itself whether the word is spelt as one word or is split into two. Both forms are equally intelligible and it is very seldom that any question of interpretation could depend on which form was used, but in an edition such as the present it is desirable that the treatment in all cases should be, so far as is possible, consistent, and it is therefore necessary at the outset to lay down certain rules which will cover at least the majority of doubtful cases. I therefore set down here my practice with regard to certain recurrent irregularities in the original texts. Even if the rules which I have followed may seem to some extent arbitrary, I can at

[1] Compare, for an exceptionally large number of examples of this sort of word-splitting, the manuscript play of *Richard II* (Malone Soc., 1929).

least plead that they have not been adopted without very careful consideration and in some cases many experiments in order to determine the most satisfactory system.

We will for the moment leave aside all the major problems of the text, errors of wording or passages which, as they stand, appear to be corrupt or meaningless, and consider how we are to treat the numerous apparent abnormalities of the early editions, with a view to determining which are to be treated as 'misprints' and corrected, and which are to be left as they stand, with or without a record of the form given to them in succeeding editions.[1] They may be divided into orthographical irregularities and grammatical irregularities.

ORTHOGRAPHICAL IRREGULARITIES

(a) *Abnormal spellings.* Certain spellings, such as 'ceaze' (seize), 'pearce' (pierce), and the famous 'Scilens' (Silence), which occur in early texts would probably not have been used by a trained scribe and would have been corrected by a careful proof-reader, at any rate if he had found them in a piece of serious literature, and to this extent they are not normal. On the other hand, at a time when spelling was only beginning to be fixed, few persons, if any,[2] would have regarded them as definitely wrong, while furthermore they are often of interest as possibly representing some individual peculiarity in the manuscript used as copy. Obviously, such things cannot be considered as 'misprints' and in an edition which does not attempt to normalize must be left as they stand.[3]

Further, provided that the context of such peculiar spellings appears to be sound, there will generally be no need to record the spelling of other editions, unless some point of interpretation is involved.[4] Comment or explanation will, if thought necessary, be included in the explanatory notes.

[1] I shall later have a good deal to say on the giving, or not giving, of collations in general, but it is convenient to anticipate a little here and indicate at once what is done with regard to these numerous minor abnormalities which would naturally be 'corrected' by later texts.

[2] Other than those 'professionally' concerned with orthography, such as schoolmasters, scribes, proof-readers, and compositors!

[3] There are, of course, a number of colloquial expressions which can hardly be said to have any regular spellings at all, such as 'birlady', 'godigoden', &c. These are naturally preserved as they occur, without comment.

[4] An abnormal spelling may, of course, sometimes rouse a suspicion that some other word was intended, and in that case it may be desirable to record whether the spelling was, or was not, retained in the earlier reprints.

(*b*) *Incorrect choice of full and contracted verbal and other forms* (*'long'* *and 'short' spellings*). We may find, for example, such various forms as

> blessed, blest; payed, paid; doest, do'st, dost; charged, charg'd, chargd; darest, dar'st, darst; wouldest, would'st, wouldst; banished, banish'd, banisht; middest, mid'st, midst.

These different spellings, which we may call 'long' and 'short', no doubt could be, and generally were, used to indicate differences of pronunciation, the termination in the one case forming a separate syllable and in the other being fused with the stem.[1] Nevertheless, in the case at any rate of Shakespeare's plays, their use was by no means consistent. A glance at the collations given in the Cambridge edition will show how frequently editors have found it necessary, in order to mark the rhythm of the lines as they understood it, to substitute a long for a short spelling or vice versa. Actually I doubt whether either author or compositor was greatly concerned to assist readers to scan the lines by this means. Shakespeare was writing for actors who were well accustomed to speaking verse, and I cannot but think that he would have expected them to speak his lines as sense and dramatic propriety required without any such adventitious aids as these. Furthermore, experience shows that if one attempts to improve the metre of lines by juggling with long and short spellings, one will often find (1) that the line can be read perfectly well as it stands by dwelling upon or by slurring some other word or syllable, or (2) that it contains two or more words which possessed both long and short spellings and that while a change of any one would give the desired smoothing of rhythm there is no reason for changing one rather than another. I have therefore thought it best in all such cases to let the spelling of the original stand and to leave the reader to read the lines as his ear tells him they should be read.[2]

(*c*) *Use and omission of apostrophes.* Many verbal forms which do

---

[1] If, however, the 'st' termination is added to a verb normally ending in e, such as 'come', giving 'comest', I doubt if this would necessarily have been regarded as calling for a disyllabic pronunciation. So too a man who habitually spelt 'do' might write the second person singular as 'dost', while one who wrote 'doe' might spell the same part of the verb as 'doest', both intending the word to be pronounced, in the usual way, as a monosyllable.

[2] As I do not regard the readings given as incorrect, I do not ordinarily record the alterations of later editions. In a few cases I have, however, recorded the readings of earlier 'reported' texts, as these may give some indication of how the lines were actually spoken on the stage.

not seem normally to have been spelt with an apostrophe, at least in the best printing-houses of the time, are occasionally given them in Shakespearian texts.[1] These include such present tenses as 'put's', 'do's', 'go's', 'can'st', and some past tenses such as 'was't', 'wer't'. There are also other analogous forms such as 'whil'st', 'among'st', ''erst', 'By'th'way', 'To'th'discontented Members', &c. These differ from the 'long' and 'short' spellings referred to under (b) in that although the apostrophe was doubtless intended to represent an elision, there were no long forms in use at the time and the apostrophe is therefore meaningless. The apostrophe occurs, however, commonly in these words in manuscripts and cannot therefore be regarded as incorrect. It is therefore retained in this text whenever it occurs in such words, but no collations are given. It is generally dropped by the Third Folio, if not earlier.

The apostrophe is also often found misplaced, as in the very frequent spelling 't'is' for ''tis', which is so common that it might almost be regarded as regular.

On the other hand, the apostrophe is frequently absent from certain contracted forms which in later times always have it; of such are

where = whether (*mod. eds.* whe're)
eer = ever (e'er)
whoes *or* whose = who is (who's)
ant = an(d) it (an't)
wast = was it (was't)
wert = were it (were't)
tis = it is ('tis)
toot = to it (to't)

All these were perfectly allowable forms at their time and are of course retained. I have therefore not recorded the alterations of the later editions, which are merely modernizations. If, however, there is doubt as to the meaning of a word (e.g. if it is possible to take 'where' either as 'where' or 'whether') an explanatory note is given.

The apostrophe, it may be noted, is also frequently omitted when the final e of the definite article is elided: e.g. 'i'th heele', 'i'th bill', 'i'th right' (*T. of S.*, IV. i. 106, IV. iii. 141, 150). Omissions of this kind may sometimes be due to mere carelessness, but their occurrence in manuscript and the fact that of the examples just cited the first was not 'corrected' until F4 and the second and third until Rowe,

---

[1] This practice seems to be particularly prevalent in the late Jacobean period. Hundreds of apostrophes were added in the First Folio texts set up from Quartos.

make it evident that we cannot regard the omission as a misprint. In cases such as the above I therefore follow my copy-text. I should, however, regard the omission of an apostrophe within a word where the spacing makes it look as if an apostrophe was intended (e.g. 'vnsur d', *K. John*, II. i. 471; 'unsur'd', F2) as due to typographical error and correct accordingly.

During the whole period of the original publication of Shakespeare's texts the apostrophe was, of course, commonly omitted in the possessive case, e.g. 'a mans life', 'Cæsars honour', 'the soldiers valour', with the result that a possessive singular, a nominative plural, and a possessive plural may be identical and that there is no means of determining, except by the general sense of the passage, whether such a phrase as 'our Glories ouerthrow' is to be interpreted as 'our Glory's overthrow' or 'our Glories' overthrow'. There is, however, nothing wrong with the phrase as it stands, and if it is desirable to indicate which of two interpretations later editions have preferred (for a modernized text must of course choose one or the other) this is a matter for the explanatory notes and not for the collations. The modernizations are glosses, not variant readings.

Another feature of the early texts should perhaps be mentioned here: namely, the omission of the possessive s before or after a sibilant; e.g. 'the Duchesse Gold', 'the Duchesse Wracke' (*2 Hen. VI*, I. ii. 87, 105), 'my Vnckle *Clarence* angry Ghost' (*Rich. III*, III. i. 144). The practice is, of course, variable; in *The Comedy of Errors*, for example, 'God sake' is found twice (I. ii. 93, V. i. 33) to three occurrences of 'Gods sake' (II. i. 76, II. ii. 24, V. i. 36). Here too, I have necessarily preserved the forms of my copy-text and have not, of course, added the apostrophe, or the apostrophe with s, that is customary in modernized editions.

(*d*) *Use of hyphens.* The use of the hyphen was much less fixed even than at present, when there is still much variation in practice. In general there is no reason at all for failing to follow the original, whatever it may be, but in one point the usage of the First Folio seems in the light of present-day practice definitely wrong, namely in a certain tendency when in a line one or more pairs of words are correctly hyphened to use hyphens between other words without logical grounds.[1] For example, in *Richard III*, II. ii. 112, F1 has

You clowdy-Princes, & hart-sorowing-Peeres

[1] There has always been a difficulty about hyphens, and our present practice of

where the hyphens after 'clowdy' and 'sorowing' are quite unusual and would even in the seventeenth century have been rejected by the more careful proof-correctors as superfluous or incorrect. We can, however, scarcely regard such things as misprints, and it seems on the whole better to let them remain. In view, however, of the uncertainty in the use of hyphens at all periods, collations of later texts are given.

Conversely, the hyphen now usual in compound epithets is frequently omitted by the early texts and I do not, of course, normalize their practice. Should there have arisen any difference of opinion as to whether the first of a pair of adjectives was adverbial or adjectival in force (as in *K. John*, I. i. 38, where the phrase 'fearefull bloudy issue' has given rise to variant readings) I should, of course, record these in the explanatory notes (see pp. 64–5). For the most part, however, explanation of such phrases is quite unnecessary as the meaning intended is clear from the context.

(*e*) *Unusual or alternative word-division.* We frequently find such words as 'grandfather', 'nobleman', 'goodman', 'nobody', 'another', 'altogether' spelt as two words, 'grand father', &c., though the sense is clearly what we should now express by the single word; and it is impossible to regard these spellings as misprints. Even, however, in Elizabethan times it seems probable that a difference was recognized between the two forms, at least in pronunciation if not always in spelling. Thus if, after Hamlet had removed the corpse of Polonius, Claudius had looked behind the arras and had remarked 'There is no body there' the way in which he uttered the words 'no body' (whether as a 'dactyl' or as an 'amphibrach') would have depended upon whether he knew that Polonius had just been killed there or not. When two words are used, however, in the sense of the modern single words, e.g. when 'noble man' is used of rank without any suggestion of nobility of character, it seems clear in view of contemporary manuscript usage that we should treat them simply as a variant form and follow the copy-text without notes or collations. When, as also happens, one word is used where two are now customary (as in the fairly frequent appearance of 'altogether' in the sense of 'all together') my procedure is, of course, the same. As in other cases, however, if any question of meaning is involved a note is given.

The same rule is followed in the case of words having a prefix

writing 'ex-Chief Constable' and 'unself-conscious' is as illogical as anything done in former times.

which sometimes appears as part of the word and sometimes separated, e.g.

a gain, a loft, a while, a bay,[1] a clock, in stead, to day, to morrow.[2]

Other words which are treated in a similar manner are

who so, so ever, shalbe (= shall be), wilbe (= will be), it self, &c.

and those forms such as 'wert' for 'were it' which are rather contracted forms than two words written as one (see under (c)). These are regarded as perfectly normal and are retained without recording the readings of other texts.

(*f*) *The prepositions and adverbs 'of', 'off', 'to', 'too', and the article and pronoun 'the', 'thee'.*

of, off. I think that we may safely say that the late Elizabethan compositors generally recognized the difference between 'of' the preposition and 'off' the adverb, and spelt them or intended to spell them as we do now. At the same time, however, it is certain that the spellings were far less strictly differentiated in current use than they are at present, and in manuscripts of the time there seems sometimes to be little consciousness of any distinction between them.[3] While, therefore, it is quite possible that some of the instances of what, according to our present custom, would be wrong spellings of the two words are simple misprints, it is impossible to distinguish these from forms allowable or usual by Elizabethan standards. The only course therefore seems to be to follow the spelling of the copy-text in all cases, giving explanatory notes where any question of meaning arises.

to, too. Very much the same is the case with these words, save that here there seems no doubt that 'too' was sometimes used intentionally as a more emphatic form of 'to', e.g. 'For one being sued too' (*Rich. III*, IV. iv. 100). 'Too' is also commonly used in the phrase 'to it' when this is contracted to a single word (without an apostrophe), i.e. 'toot'. The reason here may be that 'tot' would not suggest the

---

[1] To be at a bay *or* at abay = to be at bay (*aux abois*).

[2] I hope to give a list of words written either as one or as two, and other lists of a similar character, in an appendix in the final volume.

[3] Occasionally there seem to be indications that 'off' was still regarded as a more stressed form than 'of', to be used, for example, when standing after a verb and not followed by a governed word. Thus Nashe has 'dreamd off', 'allowed off', 'consider off', 'assured him off', 'bee sure off', &c.; e.g. '*Greene* came oftner in print than men of iudgement allowed off' (Nashe, *Works*, ed. McKerrow, i. 329. 4–5).

normal pronunciation and might be unintelligible. When the apostrophe is used we find either 'to't' or 'too't'.

'Too' is also very frequently used in the phrase 'You are too blame'. The usual explanation of this is that 'in the 16–17th c. the *to* was misunderstood as *too*, and *blame* taken as *adj.* = blameworthy, culpable' (cf. *O.E.D.*, blame, *v.*, 6). This may be so, but in view of the general uncertainty as to the distinction in spelling between the two words more evidence seems desirable. If 'blame' had commonly been regarded as equivalent to 'blameworthy' we should have expected to find such phrases as 'You are blame in this matter', which, so far as I have observed, do not occur.

The spelling 'two' is also occasionally found for the adverb or the separated preposition—not, I think, for the preposition standing before a governed word. Though this seems on the whole most likely to be a simple misprint it is difficult to be certain and I have therefore treated it in the same way as 'too'.

As in the case of 'of, off', I keep the spelling of the copy-text, whether 'to', 'too', or 'two', without any note unless some ambiguity is involved.

the, thee. While the definite article is, in printed texts, so rarely spelt 'thee' that it is natural to regard examples of this as misprints, the spelling 'the' for the pronoun of the second person is by no means uncommon, e.g. *Richard II*, v. ii. 11, 17,

> Whilst all tongues cried, God saue the Bullingbrooke . . .
> Iesu preserue the welcome Bullingbrooke . . .

and there are a number of cases—which may even include the lines quoted above—where it may be doubtful whether the article or the pronoun was intended by the compositor.

In all instances when 'the' is, or may be, intended for 'thee' I have allowed it to stand, adding an explanatory note, but no collations. I have, however, corrected 'thee' to 'the' in the very few cases in which the former stands for the definite article, noting, of course, the original reading.

(*g*) *Foreign phrases.* A special difficulty occurs with the scraps of French, Italian, and Spanish—or what seem to be intended for such —which appear in many of the plays. These are seldom, if ever, correctly spelt and sometimes appear in so corrupt a form that it is impossible to be certain what was intended. For example, we have such things as

> *vemchie, vencha, que non te vnde, que non te perreche* (*L.L.L.*, iv. ii. 91–2)

which has been restored in modern editions (from Florio's *Second Fruits*) to

Venetia, Venetia, chi non ti vede, non ti pretia;

or, to cite other examples at random, we have '*vnboyteene verd*' (*M. Wives*, I. iv: F438)[1] which should be '*vn boitier vert*', or '*La fin Corrone les eumenes*' (*2 Hen. VI*, v. ii. 28), i.e. '*la fin couronne les œuvres*'.

It may be presumed that at any rate the simpler phrases—*Qui est là?* (*Che la.*, F1), *Mi perdonate* (*Me Pardonato*, F1), *un garçon* (*oon Garsoon*, F1), and so on—had been picked up orally by the author and these were probably written down according to what seemed to be their sound, the compositor no doubt making what he could of words quite unfamiliar to him and perhaps in not too clear a script. The longer phrases may for the most part have either been learnt in a similar way or Shakespeare may have laid under contribution some travelled friend and have jotted down a rough impression of what he had been told. It would have mattered little how such phrases were spoken on the stage, for in general the intention was clearly no more than to suggest foreign speech—there was perhaps no real need that it should be intelligible even to the few who were capable of understanding it.

Now it may be argued that such phrases in the printed text probably reproduce more or less faithfully what was in the copy (with the exception perhaps of such simple mistakes as a 'u' for an 'n' and the like), and that therefore this should be retained as it stands. There is indeed much to be said for this view in certain cases: for example, 'oon garsoon' may well have been Shakespeare's way of writing 'vn garçon'—it is at least improbable. that had 'vn' been in the manuscript it would have been transformed by the compositor into 'oon'. On the other hand, we can hardly suppose that an author who knew the meaning of his quotation could have written '*vencha*' or '*vemchie*' for '*Venetia*'; it is far more likely that a compositor ignorant of the sense would misread a carelessly written '*Venetia*', which, if the word were written, as one would expect, in Italian script, might easily be done.

[1] For 'F438' compare p. 61. Where reference is necessary to plays of this edition not yet in type, and the fact of a scene being either wholly or partly in prose makes precise reference to the line number within the scene impossible, I have cited the Folio line number in the above manner. As explained below in the same context, I am including in this edition, as well as the customary line numbering within the scenes, a line numbering throughout the play based on the First Folio edition.

The truth is, I think, that we cannot in these foreign phrases even attempt to distinguish between errors or individual spellings of the author, which should be preserved, and mistakes of transmission, which should be corrected. It is therefore not unreasonable that we should follow whatever practice seems most convenient, and this is clearly that the form printed should be intelligible to the reader. I have, therefore, in all cases of the kind attempted to give such phrases in a form and spelling which would have been regarded as allowable at the date of the text, noting, however, what is found in the original edition, and, when editors have interpreted the phrase differently, the various readings given by them.

The case of Latin quotations is somewhat different, for here any errors or departures from the customary spelling are much more likely to be simple misprints of the compositor. The same rule will, however, apply to these: they are to be corrected and the original reading recorded.

GRAMMATICAL IRREGULARITIES

There are, as is generally recognized, a certain number of grammatical irregularities in the early Shakespearian texts which are as a rule replaced in the succeeding editions by forms regarded as more correct. It is quite clear that many of these departures from what we now regard as standard grammar cannot be 'misprints' but must have been in the manuscript used as copy, and there can therefore be no question of altering them in a conservative text. Indeed, there is abundant evidence that they were regarded as quite allowable in Shakespeare's time, and it is therefore not even necessary to notice the attempts of seventeenth- and eighteenth-century editors to bring the text into accordance with the practice of their own day. Of such may be instanced the double superlative ('most highest', &c.), the double negative ('nor never', &c.), and the omission of one adverbial suffix where two adverbs are joined together ('plain and bluntly', 'bitterly and strange', &c.).

It is, however, much more difficult to know how best to treat certain other grammatical forms which are not in accord with usual London English of the date.

Of these are certain inflections of the second-person singular present: (a) in -s; e.g. thou loves, gives, sets, sends (for lovest, givest, settest, sendest), and (b) a few miscellaneous anomalous forms or usages, such as 'hath' for 'hast', 'doth' for 'dost'.

Of the first of these groups it may be said that in -d and -t stems the -s termination seems to be normal at the date (the -st form being rather of the nature of a sophistication), presumably on account of the awkwardness of such forms as 'standst', 'letst',[1] which even if spelt were probably seldom spoken. The -s ending where the stem does not end in a dental may be due to analogy with the euphonic forms or may illustrate the tendency, observable in the second group ('hath' for 'hast', &c.), to level the endings of the second-person singular under the third. Sometimes, however, in the second group there may simply be a false concord comparable to the false concords of the third-person singular discussed below.

(c) Besides the above there are certain cases of the apparent use of a singular verb with a plural noun such as

Thy tough Commixtures melts (3 Hen. VI, ii. vi. 6)

His Currish Riddles sorts not with . . . (3 Hen. VI, v. v. 26).

Such forms are, of course, quite common both in print and manuscript, though they seem scarce in the books from the better printing-houses and in those in which special care seems to have been taken with the work.[2] Their origin seems still to be a matter of dispute. The latest writer on the subject, Dr. H. T. Price of the University of Michigan, calls it a 'northern plural',[3] and this has indeed been the usual name for it, though Professor Wyld considers it a misnomer.[4] Now if the only singular for plural irregularities were such cases as 'melts' for 'melt', we should I think naturally regard all such forms as a matter of differences of inflexion and take it that 'melts' actually was a plural form alternative to 'melt'. We find, however, quite a number of examples of the undoubted 'false concord' of a plural subject with a singular verb. Thus in Richard II, ii. ii. 14–15, we have the lines

---

[1] I called attention to the frequency of these -s forms in my edition of Nashe (vol. v, p. 199) in 1910, where I accepted them as normal.

[2] Much has been written on these present plurals in -s. There is, for example, a good discussion of the subject in Jacob Knecht, Die Kongruenz zwischen Subjekt und Prädikat und die 3. Person Pluralis Praesentis auf -s im elisabethanischen Englisch, Heidelberg, 1911 (reviewed by Max Förster in Sh. Jahrbuch, 48 (1912), 327–8). These -s plurals were found most frequently in the period 1580–1620. By the time of the Second Folio (1632) they seem definitely to have gone out of favour and by 1640 to have been regarded as vulgar.

[3] Journal of English and Germanic Philology, xxxvi (1937), p. 161. It is not, however, clear that Dr. Price would accept this name for it. The passage referred to occurs in an interesting article entitled 'Towards a Scientific Method of Textual Criticism for the Elizabethan Drama'.

[4] A History of Modern Colloquial English, 1936, p. 334.

> Each substance of a griefe hath twenty shadowes,
> Which shewes like griefe it selfe, but is not so:

where 'shewes' *might* be a plural in -es, but 'is' is certainly singular.
In the same play, III. ii. 141, we have

> Is Bushie, Greene, and the Earle of Wiltshire dead . . .

where again there can be no question of an -es plural. Conversely,
though far less frequently, we find a singular subject with a plural
verb, at times evidently due to lack of grammatical analysis of the
relationship between noun and verb; e.g.

> Mens flesh preseru'd so whole, doe seldome winne (*2 Hen. VI*, III. i. 301)
> 'Tis loue I beare thy glories make me speake (*3 Hen. VI*, II. i. 158).

These seem to indicate a real insensitiveness to the distinction between
singular and plural and may make us doubt as to what percentage of
the -s plurals show a real inflexional alternative and how many a simple
false concord. This is not perhaps from an editor's point of view a
matter of much importance in itself, but if we allow such false concords
to stand—and we cannot, in a conservative text, alter 'is' to 'are' and
vice versa—we have evidently no right to alter 'melts' to 'melt' if this
also *may* be a false concord, or indeed anything but a simple misprint.

On the other hand, it is quite possible that at least a certain percentage may be misprints and it is to be noticed that a great many
of such forms are replaced by the more normal ones at a very early
stage.[1] Editors of modernized texts have almost always corrected such
forms, as does Professor Dover Wilson, who calls them 'compositor's
grammar' (*Tempest*, I. i. 16), rather unfairly, I think, to the compositors, who, whether their efforts were to be praised or deplored, had
a very great influence in regularizing grammatical usage, as well as
spelling and punctuation, during Shakespeare's time, and in general
were neither so careless nor so ignorant as they have been painted.[2]

I have, however, felt it best to treat all these anomalous verbal
forms in the same way. It seems hardly correct to ignore them *simply*
as ordinary variant spellings, though this might perhaps be defended
as logical. I have therefore, while printing them as they stand, given
collations when they varied in texts not later than the First Folio.[3]

---

[1] A fair number are found in F1, but the majority are normalized in F2.

[2] As regards the quite respectable standard of Elizabethan printing as a whole,
see my article on 'The Elizabethan Printer and Dramatic Manuscripts' in *The
Library*, 4th Ser., xii (1931), 253–75.

[3] It is intended to include lists of these 'false concords', as well as of certain other
irregularities of the texts, in an appendix to the last volume of the plays.

I have treated in a similar manner the fairly frequent instances of case confusion in pronouns, leaving 'who' for 'whom', 'them' for 'they' in my text, and collating only such variants as are found in the early texts (the Quartos and First Folio).

In conclusion, when faced with these and similar problems, I have relied on the evidence of the works themselves in conjunction with that of contemporary writings and in particular that of manuscript plays, disregarding, of course, as any editor of an old-spelling edition necessarily must, present-day distinctions and notions of 'good' grammar. It is quite plain, from analogous irregularities found in manuscripts of the period, that compositors cannot be held generally responsible for verbal and grammatical irregularities of the kind I have been discussing: in fact, as printing-house spelling and grammar of the period were far more 'modern' than those of contemporary authors, the chances are not that irregularities have been foisted into these texts, but that many have, on the contrary, been levelled out.

ERRONEOUS AND DOUBTFUL READINGS

With the exception of the Foreign Phrases (see pp. 29–31), the abnormalities which we have been discussing, while they would automatically be altered in later editions by the normal process of modernization, cannot, as has been said, be regarded as misprints, and therefore in an edition such as the present there can be no justification for 'correcting' them. There are, however, apart from these abnormal or occasional forms, undoubted errors, words which are not 'real words', phrases that do not make, and never could have made, sense, and so on—genuine misprints, or at least failures of transmission. These, if we are to have a readable text at all, must clearly be corrected or, at least, emended into something intelligible.

But between the forms which are unusual but possible and those which are definitely impossible comes a third class, those words and locutions which we must class as doubtful, in that we cannot say with certainty whether it is possible for them to represent what the author wrote or not. A failure of transmission *may* have occurred; how are we to judge whether one has actually occurred or not? The earlier editors of Shakespeare are nowadays blamed for their constant interference. Instead of accepting the text of Shakespeare as it had come down to them, and being content with his style and metre as it stood, they altered or even rewrote his lines to suit the taste of their own day. Yet neither Pope nor any other of these editors seems to have had the least intention of improving upon Shakespeare; all they were trying to do was to restore what he had written. Assuming, or at least working on the assumption, that as Shakespeare was a great literary artist, his original manuscript must have been 'correct' grammatically and metrically, and that therefore all 'errors' which they found were due to faulty transmission, they naturally 'corrected' them.

However much a modern editor may wish for some infallible objective test of what is correct in the texts which have come down to us, there is and can be no such thing, and he can only do as Pope did and emend when he *thinks* that errors of transmission have occurred. He may indeed be aware that much which Pope considered as erroneous, and consequently altered, was by the custom of Shakespeare's time not erroneous at all, and that many of what seemed to Pope metrical deficiencies seemed so only because of his own ignorance of sixteenth-century pronunciation and word-stress. Ultimately, however, the decision whether a reading is sound,[1] and therefore to be allowed to stand, or an error of transmission and therefore, if possible, to be set right, is a matter of the editor's personal judgement, and to that extent the text of this edition, like that of all except facsimile reprints, is and must be eclectic.

If then we decide that a certain word or passage in our copy-text is corrupt and cannot represent what the author wrote, what follows? As I have already suggested, an editor who aims at reproducing his author's text not as it was actually printed, but as nearly as possible as it *would* have been printed if the printer had followed his copy correctly, must evidently try to emend it by substituting for the faulty passage what he supposes the author to have written.

In deciding what to substitute he will naturally make use of any evidence that he can find as to the author's intentions. In the case of simple verbal misprints it will often be possible to emend with almost the certainty of being correct, but there are other more doubtful cases, and for the emending of these it is usual for an editor to consult other editions.

It seems always to have been assumed by editors of Shakespeare, and indeed by most editors of old texts, irrespective of the relationship

---

[1] 'Sound' of course means no more here than 'probably intended by the author'. The question whether by any grammatical or factual standard it can be regarded as 'correct' does not arise.

which may have been established between the editions, that this is a reasonable and sound thing to do, but the matter is less simple than it may appear at first sight, and a few words must be said as to the utility of the collation of editions of Shakespeare and as to the limits of that utility.

I have already referred, in connexion with the choice of a copy-text, to the essential difference in the way in which we must regard a 'monogenous' series of texts, all of which go back to a single extant ancestor, and a 'polygenous' group, where, although ultimately all must of course have had a common ancestor, no such ancestor now exists, so that they may fall into two or more series the earliest members of which are not related to one another either as ancestor or descendant.[1] As a general rule the grouping of texts of printed books is of course 'monogenous'. There is commonly[2] only a single line of descent and in most cases the majority of the descendants are still extant. In the case of works which have come down to us as manuscripts, the 'poly-genous' grouping is the rule: there is generally no common ancestor extant, the manuscripts which have come down to us being merely the end-products of a number of divergent lines of descent.[3] It was, I believe, failure to recognize this essential difference between printed texts and manuscripts that led Pope and other early editors of Shake-speare, who were familiar with the methods of textual criticism applied, and quite rightly applied, to the Greek and Roman classics, to adopt the illogical method of collating all, or at least what they considered to be the 'best', texts and of choosing from them what they regarded as the 'best' readings.[4]

In the case of the great majority of the Shakespearian plays we have one early text which may be called 'original' in the sense that it is the earliest known and that all others extant are derived from it. This text stands at the head of a series of reprints and there is no external

---

[1] The 'monogenous' series may be considered as the equivalent of a family of father, son, grandson, great-grandson, &c., the father being still alive; the 'poly-genous' group to a family of brothers whose father is dead and each of whom may be the head of a family of his own.

[2] There are exceptions, though, apart from cases where we have definitely 'good' and 'bad' texts, these are not very numerous. The earliest texts of *Everyman* appear to have been printed from different manuscripts or from different lost editions.

[3] We may indeed have two or more manuscripts on the same line of descent, but in that case all except the earliest member of the line would as a rule be ignored in textual work.

[4] See 'The Treatment of Shakespeare's Text by his earlier Editors', *Proceedings of the British Academy*, 1933, pp. 106–7.

evidence whatever, and seldom any internal evidence of the slightest weight, that Shakespeare had any direct share in any of these reprints, or that any of the alterations found in them were due either to his intervention or to the use in preparing them of any manuscript or corrected copy with which he himself was in any way concerned.[1]

If we accept it then as a fact that in the case of a particular play Shakespeare was not in any way concerned with any of the reprints, the natural conclusion seems, at first sight, to be that in attempting to prepare a text which shall represent this play in the best attainable form, we should make use *only* of the 'original', even when that original is certainly defective, for in it is contained all that we can possibly recover of our author. It may seem that where it is necessary to assume error in the original, we, with our knowledge of Shakespeare's times and language, with our respectful and sympathetic study of his peculiarities of thought and diction, are much more likely to 'emend' him correctly than any of the evidently careless printers' readers of his own time. Can there, it may be said, be any possible use even in recording the readings of later texts which *must* be mere guesses at the truth? If any one is to guess, why not we ourselves?

Consideration shows, however, I think, that such an attitude towards the derived texts is not altogether reasonable. Even nowadays does the first edition of a work always represent quite perfectly what the author intended? We know that writers are often careless; even if their original manuscript is free from slips of the pen, which is seldom the case, they may employ incompetent typists, their printers may make misprints, and they may fail to read their proofs or read them carelessly. We must admit, of course, that a modern 'original' edition will generally be very close to the author's intention and that errors will generally be very few and unimportant. In respect of accuracy it is a very different thing from a sixteenth-century Quarto. At the same time we recognize the possibility of error, and that such errors may be corrected, even without the intervention of the author, in a second edition. If then we imagine a work of the present day to be scientifically edited by someone 300 years or so in the future, should we not feel that such an editor would be, as a rule, wiser if, in

---

[1] I have referred on p. 17, above, to the possibility of authentic corrections getting into certain of the later texts from the use, in reprinting, of a copy which had been corrected for theatrical purposes. But it is, I fear, at best a possibility!

cases of obvious error, and even sometimes when the sense or an allusion was obscure, he accepted the corrections of a reprint a year or two later than the original, even though he had no proof that such corrections emanated from the author—even indeed if he had proof that they did not—than if he simply ignored them and inserted in their place what it seemed to his three-hundred-year-later judgement that his author ought to have said?[1]

Of course such a comparison must not be unduly pressed, for the circumstances are very different, but it is surely arguable that *when the text of an author is obviously corrupt*, the emendation of a contemporary has at least a claim to consideration, for it will almost certainly be something which made sense at the time and *might* be the correct reading.

But there is furthermore another reason why it is unwise to ignore the early reprints, namely that they may serve to some extent as a *check* on the originals. Suppose, for example, we find a reprint consistently correcting obvious errors in a certain play, and we then come across a passage which seems to us unintelligible and which we are inclined to consider as corrupt; and suppose that here the reprint does *not* make any change. Is it not at least worth considering whether this passage may not be correct, and our failure to understand it be due to our having lost the key to some topical allusion or to our ignorance of some cant phrase which rendered it perfectly intelligible at the time? Every year sees some new phrase put into circulation, perhaps by its occurrence in a popular song, or owing to its use by members of the 'smart' set, or by a well-known actor or film-star, and such phrases spread through the various classes of the community until they are recognized to be commonplace or vulgar and are dropped.

Account must therefore, I think, be taken of at any rate the earlier Quartos and of the First Folio, and their readings must be considered.

---

[1] The point may perhaps be made clearer by an imaginary example. Supposing that in an edition of a farce or pantomime written about 1920 there occurred the phrase 'Yes, we have now bananas', a press corrector of the present day in charge of a reprint would at once recognize the meaningless popular phrase intended, and correct 'now' to 'no'. An editor of a hundred years hence, reprinting the play as a monument of Georgian literature, would (unless we suppose that editors of the twenty-first century will have a far better knowledge of the popular locutions of our own day than we have of those of Shakespeare's time) be far more likely to retain the text as it stood and to add a note on the popularization of the banana in England in the early years of the century.

To what extent it is necessary to record the readings of these and other editions will be discussed below (pp. 63–73).

The general principles followed in the formation of the text and the extent to which emendation is permitted having been discussed, there remain, I think, only two special points to be mentioned here.

One is that, although the edition chosen as copy-text is followed, as I have explained, as closely as possible, I have in certain cases felt obliged to insert in their place passages or complete scenes from editions earlier or later than the copy-text; for example, the so-called 'deposition scene' of *Richard II* (IV. i. 154–318), which is first found in Q4, a whole scene of *Titus Andronicus* (III. ii), first printed in F1, and the 'Iacke' lines in *Richard III* (IV. ii. 100–19), which only occur in the Quartos. These have come to be regarded as essential parts of the plays, and although in some cases, e.g. the *Titus Andronicus* scene, it is at least open to doubt whether they are not the work of another hand, it would be very inconvenient to relegate them to an appendix. Such passages are enclosed in square brackets as a special warning of their absence from the copy-text. They are of course given in the spelling and with the punctuation of the edition from which they are taken.

The other point is that so far as possible all corrections are given in the form which involves the smallest departure from what is printed in the text, on the assumption that this is the form which the word is most likely to have had in the author's manuscript. Thus in a passage already cited from *The Comedy of Errors*, I. ii. 65–7, the First Folio has

> For she will scoure your fault vpon my pate:
> Me thinkes your maw, like mine, should be your cooke,
> And strike you home without a messenger.

In the first two lines the words 'scoure' and 'cooke' have been emended by Rowe and Pope respectively to 'score' and 'clock', and the emendations appear to have been universally approved. In inserting them into my text I give them, however, in the forms 'scoare' and 'clocke', these being, in view of the existing text, the forms which they seem most likely to have had in the manuscript.

Besides the correction of verbal misprints, I have made certain deviations from the original in punctuation and in line arrangement. Of each of these kinds of editorial interference something must be said.

PUNCTUATION

As regards punctuation my rule has been to allow this to remain unaltered whenever, though perhaps insufficient or careless, it is not clearly *mistaken*.[1]

By 'mistaken', however, I do not mean at all what we should now call incorrect. There are innumerable cases in which the punctuation is, from a syntactic point of view, quite wrong, at least according to modern ideas. I believe, however, that in very many of these cases a reader will find that if he reads the text in a natural manner the pauses which he makes will correspond closely to the punctuation, and in others that though *he* would perhaps not read it quite in this way, it *can* be so read, especially when we take into account the possibility of a certain amount of action. And if there is a way of uttering the text—even though it be not our usual way—which corresponds with the punctuation, it appears to me that it would be definitely wrong to alter it.

To take, almost at random, a single example: in *3 Henry VI*, II. vi. 51–8, the First Folio has:

> *War.* From off the gates of Yorke, fetch down yᵉ head, 51
> Your Fathers head, which *Clifford* placed there:
> In stead whereof, let this supply the roome, 53
> Measure for measure, must be answered.
>
> *Ed.* Bring forth that fatall Schreechowle to our house, 55
> That nothing sung but death, to vs and ours:
> Now death shall stop his dismall threatning sound, 57
> And his ill-boading tongue, no more shall speake.

Now in this passage a modern text would omit the commas within lines 51, 53, 54, 56, and 58, but every one of these corresponds to a natural pause,[2] and is in some measure an actual help in the reading of the lines. In three cases at least, lines 51, 56, and 58, where alterna-

---

[1] I have, however, allowed myself to emend the punctuation silently in one respect. There are a very large number of cases in which there is either no punctuation at all, or a comma, at the end of a completed speech or of a stage direction, where a full point is undoubtedly required. This can only be due to carelessness, to the stop falling away in the course of printing, or to a shortage of type, and has no possible significance. I have therefore in all such cases supplied the stop without noting its absence (or the presence of a comma) in the original. This, of course, does not apply to speeches left incomplete either owing to the interruption of another speaker or by aposiopesis; in such cases any alteration is noted.

[2] Remembering the necessities of theatrical declamation. This is a speech in an open theatre, not a quiet conversation in a room.

tive pauses are possible, it indicates the correct one. The actor must
not say

> From off the gates—of Yorke fetch down yᵉ head,

or

> That nothing sung—but death to vs and ours:

or

> And his ill-boading—tongue no more shall speake.

Nor on the other hand must he say

> In stead whereof let this—supply the roome,

or

> Measure for measure must—be answered.

It may be objected that even without the commas no one would
read the lines wrongly: and this may be true, at least of us nowadays.
But if the text was written with a definite verse-cadence in the writer's
mind which he wished to be retained in the actors' utterance, why
should he not have indicated it? And if he did so, or *may have done
so*, are we justified in ignoring what may be the evidence of it? I
think not.

And even if we find, as we do, cases in which no such care seems
to have been taken with the punctuation, is this an argument for
abandoning it when it does seem to have been careful? Again, I
think not.

In any case there can be no good reason for modernizing punctuation in a text which does not modernize the spelling, for the one is
just as likely to preserve characteristics of the author's manuscript as
the other. Nevertheless we must, as in the case of any other misprint,
correct the punctuation when, by Elizabethan practice, it is clearly
erroneous, especially if it is so far wrong that it might mislead a
reader. Unfortunately the subject of punctuation is one which bristles
with difficulties, and there is still much work to be done before it will
be possible to say what usages would have been regarded, by an
educated Elizabethan, as allowable and what would have been regarded as definitely wrong. Throughout the period there seems to
have been in progress a gradual change-over from a method of
punctuation based simply upon the natural pauses made in reading
to one which took account mainly of the logical relationship of the
parts of a sentence, with the natural result of much confusion between
the two systems. In an appendix in the last volume I hope to collect
a certain number of examples illustrating the practice, so far as there

can be said to be one, of the Shakespearian texts. In the meantime I need only say that in the majority of texts, at any rate in those that are printed from the First Folio, it will, I think, be found that though the punctuation may at first seem somewhat strange, and though it is undoubtedly less regular than we are accustomed to nowadays, it really presents no more difficulty to the reader than the old spelling does, while it often suggests the way in which a speech is intended to be uttered more clearly than does the more 'logical' punctuation of the modern texts.

There is, however, one type of irregular punctuation which I have felt bound to alter, namely those rather numerous cases in which a clause is separated by a major stop, such as a semicolon, colon, or full point, from another to which it logically belongs, while at the same time it is only separated by a comma from one with which it has much less close logical connexion.

Thus, for example, in *3 Henry VI*, v. iii. 22–4, the Folio has

And as we march, our strength will be augmented:
In euery Countie as we goe along,
Strike vp the Drumme, cry courage, and away. *Exeunt*.

Here the sense intended is evidently that King Edward's strength will be augmented in every county as he marches along; while the punctuation, if given the force that we now give to it, would make the passage an injunction to strike up the drum, cry courage, and away, in every county through which they march, which is clearly absurd!

Now one can of course easily invent a theory that the colon had not the force that it now has and that it was used in some way to *connect* clauses or phrases rather than to separate them,[1] and one could, no doubt, find examples, even numerous ones, to support such a theory. On the other hand, we should find a far larger number of cases in which the colon is used, as we use it now, to separate parts of a sentence each of which is more or less complete in itself, and this is approximately the explanation of its use given by the grammarians of Shakespeare's time.[2] It appears to me that these rather curious transpositions of comma and semicolon may, at least in many cases, arise from a proof-corrector marking a colon in a passage

[1] Cf. the present use of the colon after 'namely'.
[2] '*Colon* is noted by two round points one aboue another, which in writing followeth som full branch, or half the sentence, as *Tho the daie be long: yet at the last commeth euensong*', Mulcaster, *Elementarie*, M3ᵛ; cf. also Jonson, *Grammar* (*Works*, ed. Cunningham, ix. 317–18).

originally punctuated only by commas, and the compositor then accidentally placing it at the end of the wrong line, a thing by no means difficult to do. It is, I think, commoner to find the misplaced colon at the end of a line than intermediate in it.

As, further, this 'misplacement', or if one prefers it 'unusual placing', of the colon occurs much more frequently in some texts than in others, and as in most cases the punctuation is corrected in an early reprint to one in accordance with our present custom, I have treated it as an error and altered it, giving in all cases the reading of my copy-text in a footnote.

As will be seen, my general principle in dealing with this and similar difficulties of punctuation has been so far as possible, and always when no serious ambiguity can arise, to keep the original punctuation within a clause, but to change it when, as it stands, it might give a misleading impression of the interrelationship of the various clauses within a sentence.

Queries. In a very large number of cases we find that rhetorical questions are closed by a full point when we more commonly use a query. There seem too many of these for us to regard them as ordinary misprints, and it seems safest to suppose that *when no answer was expected* the phrase was regarded rather as an exclamation than a question in spite of its having the form of the latter. Thus in *1 Henry VI*, v. iv. 147–50, we have

> Insulting *Charles*, hast thou by secret meanes
> Vs'd intercession to obtaine a league,
> And now the matter growes to compremize,
> Stand'st thou aloofe vpon Comparison.

This is, of course, formally a question. Actually, however, it has the force of an accusation rather than a question, and if an author or his printer chose so to regard it, it seems hardly for us to force upon him grammar rather than meaning. As in any case none of these stops can cause the slightest ambiguity, I keep them.

A few other points concerning the punctuation of the early texts may here be noted. We find in the early texts that the interrogation mark is frequently placed after the question proper, rather than at the end of the period as is now customary; that sentences which are properly exclamatory (especially those introduced by 'what', 'how', &c.) are pointed with a query; that interrupted speeches are, with very few exceptions, terminated with a period, and that, on the other hand, completed sentences are at times linked by commas where modern usage would demand a much heavier stop. It is impossible to be certain how far some of these features (especially that last mentioned) are merely printers' errors, or in general to assess the relative responsibility of author and printer for the pointing of the texts. It is, however, quite certain that if an editor should attempt to normalize the punctuation according to any system or supposed system of the Elizabethans—whether writers or printers—there would be no end to the undesirable tampering which his theories would lead him to inflict on his text. I have, therefore, in all such cases of abnormality allowed the copy-text pointing to stand unless, of course, it is either definitely wrong or liable to misinterpretation.

LINE ARRANGEMENT

There appears nothing to be gained by too slavish an adherence to the line distribution of the early editions, for it is clear that many passages are there printed as prose which were intended as verse, while on the other hand what is undoubtedly prose is often printed in lines which do not fill the type-measure and are capitalized as verse. The early editors, especially Pope, rearranged many such passages with evident advantage, and later editors have, as I think rightly, followed them.

At the same time, however, there are many passages in which it is difficult to be certain whether prose or verse was intended. It is, of course, often very easy to force a line into verse by comparatively slight changes, especially by the adjustment of long and short verbal forms ('blessed' and 'blest', and so on) or by assuming elision of syllables (reading 'dangerous' as 'dang'rous', &c.), a practice to which Pope was greatly addicted; but in a conservative text the wisdom of such tampering is, to say the least of it, questionable. The truth is no doubt that, at least in dramatic writing, there was no clear and consistent distinction between verse and prose, and that in many cases a more or less rhythmical prose took the place of formal verse. In particular, little regard, even in what is clearly verse, seems to have been paid to the formation of complete lines. There are a number of passages consisting of an uneven number of part-lines in which little difference is made metrically if we begin with a part-line or if we rearrange the passage throughout so as to end with one.

Perhaps the most difficult of the problems which concern metre is how to treat the short lines which often occur in rapid interchange of speech. The usual arrangement in the early texts was to give a separate line to each speech,[1] taking no regard of the metrical structure, if any. Thus, in *Two Gentlemen*, I. ii (F201–3), we have

> *Lu.* To plead for loue, deserues more fee, then hate.
> *Iul.* Will ye be gon?
> *Lu.* That you may ruminate.

Here it is evident that Julia's speech and Lucetta's reply are intended to form metrically a single line. This was no doubt always recognized by editors and all intelligent readers of Shakespeare, but no attempt was made to indicate it typographically until Steevens's edition of 1793, when the lines were printed thus:

> *Luc.* To plead for love deserves more fee than hate.
> *Jul.* Will you be gone?
> *Luc.*   That you may ruminate.

This fashion has continued until the present time, at any rate in texts in which the lines are numbered according to metrical units.

In a few early texts, however, in particular the Quartos of Ben Jonson's plays, the system was adopted of printing metrical lines always as typographical units. Thus in *Volpone*, II. i. 34–5, in a dialogue between Peregrine and Politique Would-Bee, the text of the 1616 Quarto runs:

> PER. Yes, and your lyons whelping, in the *Tower*.
> POL. Another whelpe! PER. Another, sir. POL. Now, heauen!

This system was abandoned in the Jonson Folio, and though it is occasionally found in later plays it never became very common in England.

The modern editors have, as a general rule, tended to treat all lines which *could* be metrical, or could be *made* metrical by a slight alteration, as verse and to print them as such. When therefore they meet with short lines forming part of consecutive speeches which *can* be made into a line, they do the same with these and throw the second one over to the right as in the *Two Gentlemen* lines referred to above, which, if we are differentiating prose and verse by the setting-out in print, seems logical.

---

[1] Occasionally two short speeches were placed on the same line, apparently for economy of space, or in some cases possibly to make room for corrections in type.

The difficulty lies, of course, in deciding what is prose and what is verse, inasmuch as consecutive speeches cannot by any means always be put together into such perfect lines as 'Will you be gone? That you may ruminate.' For example, in *Richard II*, v. ii, we find a number of these doubtful lines, some of which modern editors have treated as prose while others hardly more metrical have been printed as verse; thus:

> *Yor.* Giue me my bootes I say.
> *Du.* Why Yorke what wilt thou doe?   (ll. 87–8)

The above is generally printed as prose in modern editions, though the scene is for the most part in verse. On the other hand, speeches no more metrical than this are treated as verse. Thus in the Cambridge edition we find

> *York.* . . . I fear, I fear,—
> *Duch.*   What should you fear?   (l. 64)
> *York.* . . . I will appeach the villain.
> *Duch.*   What is the matter?   (l. 79)
> *York.* . . . To kill the king at Oxford.
> *Duch.*   He shall be none.   (l. 99)

It seems to me very difficult to maintain that there is any real distinction here as between prose and verse. There is perhaps something a little more prosaic in York's request for his boots than in some of the other dialogue, but *metrically* the line begins well, and if the rest of it is a foot too long, why, so is 'What is the matter?' in l. 79, while l. 64 is a foot too short. For my own part I cannot see that this attempt to patch together imperfect lines has much to commend it. On the other hand, the distinction between verse and more or less rhythmical prose was in any case slight and of little importance, and there is an obvious advantage in departing as little as possible from the conventional numbering of the lines. I have therefore attempted a compromise which I do not defend as logical, but which seems to work well enough in practice and which probably comes as near as is possible to the intention of the author. This principle is as follows.

When a scene as a whole is obviously intended to be verse, I assume that broken lines are probably intended to be part of the verse structure and have so treated them if this seemed at all possible, and if they had been so treated by previous editors.[1] On the other hand, in

---

[1] Pope, followed by the other eighteenth-century editors up to Johnson, generally doctored broken lines so as to make them into verse. The Cambridge and modern editors have generally retained the verse arrangement though omitting the doctoring.

prose passages I have, as a rule, only printed lines as verse if they are clearly intended to be such, as for example when they form part of a rimed proverb or of a song. Similarly, in the case of a character whose speech is generally prose, I have not printed single speeches as verse even when by a little forcing they may be so read.

As an example of prose printed in the Folio as verse, owing in all probability to the compositor having merely followed the distribution of the lines of his manuscript without thinking, I may cite a passage from *Romeo and Juliet*, IV. v. 130–2:

> *Peter.* O I cry you mercy, you are the singer.
> I will say for you, it is musique with her siluer sound,
> Because Musitions haue no gold for sounding:

Q2 and editions down to Rowe printed this passage as verse, Pope being the first to give it as prose, which—in common with the later part of the scene—it surely is. In such a clear case as this I can see no use in adhering to the evidently erroneous arrangement of the copy-text, and accordingly print as prose.

To sum up, I have as a rule, when a slight redivision of the lines would result in adequate verse, so divided them, noting the first person, generally Pope, who made this redistribution. I have, how-ever, while in general noting the later editors who agreed with the distribution which I have adopted, not always recorded the division of other editors.[1] It seems to me that the structure of dramatic verse at the period was often such that even the dramatists themselves might have found it difficult to decide between two or more possible schemes of distribution.

A curious practice of the First Folio (followed by the later ones) as regards line arrangement must be mentioned here. It occurs, I think, occasionally in almost all the plays, though it is perhaps especially frequent in *Titus Andronicus* and the three parts of *Henry VI*, and consists in printing the first line of a speech as two part-lines, even though the preceding speech has ended with a com-plete one. Thus, for example, the famous speech of York in *3 Henry VI*, I. iv. III, &c., begins thus in F1:

> *Yorke.* Shee-Wolfe of France,
> But worse then Wolues of France,
> Whose Tongue more poysons then the Adders Tooth . . .

---

[1] There are passages which might be divided, and have been divided, in a large number of different ways, and to give all these would have greatly encumbered the notes without adding anything of real value.

Now 'Shee-Wolfe . . . Wolues of France,' is, of course, metrically a single line, and, though in the Folio column there would not have been room for the whole of it, there seems no reason why it should not have been printed with a turnover:

> *Yorke.* Shee-Wolfe of France, but worse then Wolues
> of France.[1]

Other examples of the same practice are:

> *Glost.* The Church? where is it?
> Had not Church-men pray'd,
> His thred of Life had not so soone decay'd . . . (*1 Hen. VI*, I. i. 33-4)
> *Yorke.* Great Lords and Gentlemen,
> What meanes this silence? (*1 Hen. VI*, II. iv. 1)
> *Bass.* Villaine, thou knowest
> The Law of Armes is such . . . (*1 Hen. VI*, III. iv. 38)

In a certain number of cases it seems at first sight as if this arrangement might be intentional, for there is at the end of the part-line a more than usually important pause, either for emphasis or when a new person is addressed, as in

> *Lewis.* Then *Warwicke*, thus:
> Our Sister shall be *Edwards* . . . (*3 Hen. VI*, III. iii. 134)
> *Rich.* The Gates made fast?
> Brother, I like not this. (*3 Hen. VI*, IV. vii. 10)

Consideration of a large number of cases shows, however, I think, convincingly that there is as a rule no such intention in this arrangement, and we are driven to regard it as purely typographical in origin. In the majority of extant manuscripts of plays the speakers' names are written in the margin and there is therefore as much room for the first line of a speech as for any other. There can thus be no graphic reason for the practice, and if it is a matter of convenience alone it can only be due to the narrowness of the Folio column. That this is almost certainly the case can be seen by reference to the Quarto texts of those plays in which a Quarto served as copy for the Folio. By far the greatest number of examples occur in *Titus Andronicus*, where they can easily be found by reference to the collation notes. In the first scene, for example, seventeen lines which are printed as whole in the Quartos are divided into two in the Folio: ll. 9, 49, 59, 73, 168, 174, &c.

---

[1] In the *True Tragedy* it is printed as a single line with 'France' only turned over, as the Quarto type-measure is somewhat longer.

In the other plays belonging to the same category instances of this breaking of the lines in the Folio are far fewer, but they occur, and those that there are all point in the same direction; e.g.

> *Sola.* Heere comes *Bassanio,*
> Your most noble Kinsman . . . (*M. of V.*, I. i. 57)
> *Ner.* From both.
> My Lord *Bellario* greets your Grace . . . (*M. of V.*, IV. i. 120)

where Q1, from which the Folio is printed, has single lines. In many cases in *Romeo and Juliet* the Quarto has similarly a single line where the Folio prints as two; e.g. I. v. 89, II. ii. 130, and III. iii. 1.

These instances afford, I think, sufficient evidence that this peculiarity of the Folio is not based on the copy from which it was printed, and we may safely assume that it is due to the compositor alone, who may for some reason have disliked the appearance of a turnover in the first line of a speech.[1] I have therefore in all such cases printed the lines as one, following in this Pope and all later editors, though I have, of course, noted the change made.

ACCESSORIES

We may now pass to those accessories of the plays in which I have not thought it necessary to follow the copy-text exactly, but have to some extent normalized, namely act and scene divisions, stage directions, and speakers' names.

ACT AND SCENE DIVISIONS

In the Quarto editions issued before the appearance of the First Folio in 1623, none of the plays is divided into scenes, and only one, namely *Othello*, is divided into acts. In the Folio six plays are printed without divisions of any kind; one, *Hamlet*, is divided into acts and scenes (partly) as far as the beginning of II. ii, but the beginning of the third act is not marked and the rest of the play is undivided; eleven plays are divided into acts alone, the remaining eighteen into acts and scenes. As the plays fully divided in the Folio include some

---

[1] Occasionally resort may have been had to division of lines in order to avoid an awkward page-ending. Thus in *2 Hen. VI*, I. i. 203–5, three consecutive single-line speeches are split in this way. One would in any case have occupied two lines of print, but the other two need not. If, however, the printer had printed these two as single lines he would have found that the exit which follows l. 209 would have had to begin the next page, an arrangement which he may well have desired to avoid.

which were printed from undivided Quartos, it seems possible that the division was in all cases the work of the compilers of the Folio and was not found in the original manuscript.[1]

This being so, it might be argued that in a text in which an attempt is made to reproduce the plays in a form as near as possible to that in which the author left them, act and scene divisions should be ignored altogether and the plays printed without break. It seems to me, however, that such a proceeding, whether logical or not, would cause so much inconvenience to the reader that it would be unreasonable to adopt it. Whether or not the plays were originally regarded by their author as made up of five acts, each act being divided into definite 'scenes', is an arguable point, but that breaks of some sort in the performance were recognized is clear enough. As we have no means of ascertaining where Shakespeare intended these breaks to occur, it seems best to place them in those positions which the consensus of critical opinion has decided to be most suitable, and I have therefore followed, with one or two minor exceptions, the arrangement of the Cambridge editors, which is generally identical with that of Capell and which seems to have been almost universally accepted by later scholars. It would, I may say, have been in any case absolutely necessary to number the lines according to the accepted acts and scenes, for otherwise reference to the edition would have been impossible.

STAGE DIRECTIONS

While in some cases we may reasonably doubt the authority of the stage directions found in the early texts—whether, that is, they are due to the author of the play or to a member of the theatrical company by which the play was acted—it seems to me desirable that *so far as possible* the stage directions should be given in the form in which they first appear. I have therefore—even sometimes at the cost of a little awkwardness of expression—generally retained them as printed, adding within square brackets whatever seems to be absolutely necessary. I do not ordinarily use square brackets for editorial additions in the text,[2] and I do not defend them in the stage directions on

---

[1] In one case, *Titus Andronicus*, Act II, it seems as if the act division had been marked very carelessly in the Quarto used as copy-text for the Folio *after* certain stage directions had been inserted, and therefore probably immediately before printing. See introduction to that play.

[2] They are, however, as noted on p. 39, above, used to give warning of the insertion of complete lines or passages from a text other than the copy-text.

any logical grounds. They are simply a matter of convenience. If it is understood that a bracketed name or direction is not in the copy-text, this will in practice often save much space in the collation notes. It must be remembered that the change which it is necessary to make in a stage direction is most frequently an addition of a name or names omitted, and that actual correction is seldom required.

There is much variation in the early editions in the typographical form in which stage directions appear—in italic, in roman, in italic with names in roman, &c. I have as a general rule always followed the copy-text in each particular case. This necessarily introduces some lack of uniformity in the different plays, but to attempt to normalize in this respect introduces other inconsistencies. When therefore I introduce (in square brackets) a stage direction from another edition or amplify one already present, I adapt it to the convention of the copy-text, whatever this may be.

There is some difference in the practice of the various printers and editors in the use of '*Exit*', &c. As a general rule in the early texts the words '*Exit*' and '*Exeunt*' are used without the addition of a name not only when the last speaker leaves the stage but when he bids some one else to do so; in other words, when it is quite obvious who is intended to go off, it is not regarded as necessary to specify this. We may take an example at random from *Richard III*, where Buckingham sends Catesby to Gloucester to ask for an interview with him (*Rich. III*, III. vii. 88–94). Buckingham is speaking to Catesby.

> *Buck.* Sorry I am, my Noble Cousin should
> Suspect me, that I meane no good to him:
> By Heauen, we come to him in perfit loue,
> And so once more returne, and tell his Grace.   *Exit.*
> When holy and deuout Religious men
> Are at their Beades, 'tis much to draw them thence,
> So sweet is zealous Contemplation.

It is of course quite clear that the *Exit* refers to Catesby, as Buckingham continues to speak; but in cases such as this modern editors (in this instance all from Rowe onwards) generally print '*Exit Catesby*'. It appears to me that this is unnecessary and I therefore do not *add* the name of a character to whom a piece of action is prescribed when the action called for is merely the carrying out of an order contained in the text. On the other hand, if it is there in the copy-text I do not remove it. In the case of '*Exeunt*' I have similarly been guided entirely by what seemed necessary in the particular

E

case. Of course, if '*Exeunt*' is equivalent to '*Exeunt omnes*', as commonly at the end of a scene, there can be no possible use in adding the names of the characters who go off. We often, however, find a simple '*Exeunt*' in the copy-text when only part of those present on the stage are intended to leave it. In such cases if it is clearly indicated in the adjacent text who is to leave I do not add the names. Thus in *Titus Andronicus*, IV. i. 118–21, we have

> *Titus.* No boy not so, Ile teach thee another course,
> *Lauinia* come, *Marcus* looke to my house,
> *Lucius* and Ile goe braue it at the Court,
> I marrie will we sir, and weele be waited on. *Exeunt.*

Editors from Capell onwards have substituted a direction of the type of '*Exeunt Boy* [*i.e. Lucius*], *Titus, and Lavinia*', but this is surely unnecessary as no attentive reader could mistake the action intended.

Further, there are numerous cases where an associated pair or group of persons is on the stage, such as a man and his servant, or two or three friends who have entered together. If now one of such a pair or group says 'Let us go', or something to that effect, and we find the direction *Exeunt*, it is in general sufficiently obvious that this is intended to apply to the pair or group and it seems quite unnecessary to specify, as many editors do, '*Exeunt A and his servant*' or '*Exeunt A, B, and C*'. In all such cases I have gone on the general principle of not interfering with the form of the original if to leave it alone creates no ambiguity.

On the other hand, there certainly are cases when though it is quite clear on consideration or from what follows later in the scene, or sometimes later in the play, who was intended to leave the stage or to carry out some other action, this is not immediately apparent from the context. In such cases I have added, within square brackets, what seems necessary to make the matter clear.

It should be remarked that square brackets are not used in a stage direction when it is merely a matter of emending an already existing word: thus where I emend '*Exit*' to '*Exeunt*' or vice versa I do not place the emended word or any part of this in square brackets. Nor, in the few cases where the substitution of one word for another, its equivalent, is necessary do I use square brackets. Square brackets are, in fact, intended to bring to the reader's attention an editorial *addition* (see below, p. 55).

Great irregularity is found in many early texts with regard to the directions '*Exit*', '*Exeunt*', '*Manet*', and '*Manent*'. It is probable that in the original manuscripts these generally appeared in a much abbreviated form such as '*Ex.*' or '*Man.*', as indeed they were not infrequently printed. When this was the case a printer who knew a certain amount of Latin might expand them correctly to *Exit, Exeunt, Manet, Manent*, according as the action covered by the direction was of one person or more. Whether the correct form was used or not seems, however, in many early editions to have been very much a matter of chance, and we find for example innumerable cases of such false concords as

> *Exit King, Queene, and Suffolke* (2 *Hen. VI*, 1. i. 70)
> *Exit Buckingham, and Somerset* (2 *Hen. VI*, 1. i. 175)
> *Exit Warwicke, and Salisbury* (2 *Hen. VI*, 1. i. 209)
> *Manet Vernon and Basset* (1 *Hen. VI*, iii. iv. 27).

Later editions have in all cases tended to correct these false concords, and according to my rule of correcting Latin quotations when they appear to contain simple misprints (see p. 31) it might be thought that I should correct such errors as these, which probably would have been put right in a transcript made by a careful scribe. As, however, we find similar errors quite frequently in manuscript plays, we cannot be at all sure that they were not as often due to the carelessness or indifference of the author as to that of a compositor, and it seems better to leave them as they stand. The fact that '*Exit*' had become more or less anglicized would perhaps in itself account sufficiently for the irregular way in which it was often used. Further, as they can in no case introduce any ambiguity and as the correction of them is purely a formal matter, I have not thought it necessary to record corrections of them by the editors of later editions.

The various editors have added a large number of stage directions, and these—indeed even more elaborate ones than are usually given— are doubtless useful in modernized editions for the general reader. They may often assist persons lacking in visual imagination and enable them to follow the action more easily. For the purposes of the present edition, however, I feel that the less that is added to the text as originally set forth, the better. I have therefore as a rule refrained from inserting stage directions not in the copy-text when the action intended can readily be inferred from the text itself. Thus, to give a couple of instances, when in *3 Henry VI*, v. i. 11, a character says 'Then *Clarence* is at hand, I heare his Drumme', it seems to me quite unnecessary to add '*Drum heard*' as is done by Capell, followed by the later editors, even in this case by the Cambridge edition, which is comparatively sparing of such additions.[1] Nor have I thought it necessary in *Richard III*, IV. iv. 29, when the Duchess of York says 'Rest thy vnrest on Englands lawfull earth' to add, as Capell does, the direction '*sitting down on it*'.

In particular the editors have frequently added 'Attendants', 'Courtiers', 'Soldiers', &c., when the early texts simply mark the entrance of the principal persons. My practice has been only to add names of persons who actually *speak* or are individually addressed when these happen to be omitted. It may, of course, as a general rule be taken for granted that a king does not appear in state without being accompanied by a certain number of attendants—doubtless, in practice, as many as the stage would accommodate or as were available for the purpose—and that generals, however courageous, do not make an attack upon a town without at least *some* soldiers.

Thus when in *1 Henry VI*, II. i. 7, Talbot, Bedford, and Burgundy enter with scaling-ladders to attack Orleans, it is hardly to be supposed that even on the Elizabethan stage they entered alone carrying the ladders! Capell here added '*and Forces*' and later editors have followed him, but if we are to be consistent in such additions we must constantly make irritating little insertions in the directions, and it is difficult to know where to stop. Symbolism is of the essence of the drama; a fight between two captains and perhaps a couple of men could represent what in real life would be an extended combat between two large bodies of troops, and I think we may safely leave it at that.

While as a general rule I have altered the stage directions of the original as little as possible, I have, however, for the reader's convenience made occasional minor additions. When we find alternative names used for a character, such as 'Gloucester' and 'Humphrey', 'Joan' and 'Pucel', one has of course *in the text* to keep them as they are. This being so, there seems no good reason to alter them in the stage directions, as modern editors do, in order to bring them into conformity with their list of Dramatis Personae. There is, however, perhaps a certain awkwardness in an entry of, say, '*Joan*', followed immediately by '*Pucel*' as the prefix of her first speech, a discrepancy which

---

[1] It seems rather remarkable that when five lines later Edward says 'Goe, Trumpet, to the Walls, and sound a Parle' no editor apparently has thought it necessary to add '*Parle sounded*'.

occurs sometimes in the original text, and, owing to my normalization of the speakers' names, far more frequently in this edition. I
have, therefore, whenever a name *in an entry* appears in a form which
does not correspond to the normalized speaker's name, added this in
the *first case* in each scene in a bracket. See, for example, *2 Henry VI*,
I. iii. 95 S.D., where the Folio has '*Duke Humfrey*' and I have added
'[*of Gloster*]' in order to connect the entry with the speech prefix,
which is *Glost.* If the same name occurs, however, later in the
stage directions of the scene, I assume that the identity is known and
make no addition.

Asides. It is a little difficult to know what to do about 'asides'. If
none had been marked in the early texts I should have omitted such
indications altogether, leaving it to the judgement of the reader to
infer when a speech was intended to be heard by the rest of the
characters and when not. As, however, we sometimes get such indications I have thought it better to follow the usual practice and to mark
those speeches which seem supposed not to be heard by the other
characters on the stage.

It should, however, be noted that editors mark two entirely different
kinds of speeches as '*aside*', namely (1) those which are intended as
reflections of the speaker for the benefit of the audience but are not
supposed to be audible to any of the characters on the stage. These
are, of course, instances of an ancient theatrical convention which has
ceased to obtain in the serious drama. Only the villain in melodrama
now 'talks to himself' out loud. The other kind of '*aside*' (2) is when
the characters on the stage are formed into two groups, one perhaps
on the front of the stage and the other hidden or in the background
watching and commenting upon the first group. The comments are
intended to be audible to other members of the group and to the
audience, but not to those on the front of the stage. Some editors,
such as Capell and Dover Wilson, mark all the speeches of con-
cealed characters as asides, especially in elaborate eavesdropping
scenes, such as *Twelfth Night*, II. v; but the majority, I think, do not.
There seems indeed little reason for so doing, as the omission to distinguish such speeches can seldom or never cause confusion, and
some difficulty arises when, as often happens, the main part of the
action passes from the overheard to the eavesdroppers or vice versa.
I have therefore only marked as aside those speeches which seem to
be intended for the hearing of the audience alone.

Asides are in this edition indicated by a ℂ preceding the first word of the aside. When the aside does not continue to the end of the speech, its close is indicated by a 𝔻.

Further, I have often omitted the direction '*Within*' added by the later editors, partly because when a speaker was not supposed to be on the front part of the stage the fact is generally obvious, and partly because in many of such cases I doubt if the speaker was meant to be actually 'within'. With an open theatre and an audience a great part of which was not seated and was therefore necessarily much less quiet than an audience of to-day, it seems to me unlikely that a voice actually off the stage would have been audible when more was required than mere cries or shouting. Further, it would often be desirable that the audience should know who was speaking. In such cases it seems highly probable that the actor spoke from the gallery. Thus, to take an example from *1 Henry VI*, I. iii, where the Warders of the Tower answer the knocking at the door and their speeches are marked by editors '*within*', it seems much more probable that they spoke from the gallery, or perhaps, if one was available, from a window. Woodville the Lieutenant is indeed at first invisible, and here the Folio describes him as speaking '*within*', but he too may have appeared later in the gallery.

SPEAKERS' NAMES

For the reasons given on pp. 19–20, it appears to me that the varying spellings or abbreviations of the speakers' names which we find in the early editions have no authority but followed the convenience of the printer and that therefore no good purpose can be served by retaining them in anything but a facsimile reprint. Further, in many plays, apart altogether from variation in the spellings or abbreviations of the names, there is great variation in the names themselves. Thus, in *The Comedy of Errors* we find the name *Angelo* alternating with *Goldsmith*; in *Romeo and Juliet*, *Capulet* alternates with *Father*, and *Lady Capulet* with *Mother*; in *Love's Labour's Lost* the speeches of *Ferdinand* are sometimes assigned to *Nauarre* and sometimes to *King*, the *Princess of France* is alternatively *Queen*; *Armado, Holofernes, Nathaniel, Moth,*[1] *Costard*, and *Anthony Dull* are also known as *Braggart, Pedant, Curate, Boy* or *Page, Clown*, and *Constable*; and we find the same thing in many other plays. As I have argued

---

[1] Actually, as noted below, the name *Moth* never occurs in speech-prefixes; it is found only in the stage directions and dialogue (cf. p. 57, n. 3).

elsewhere,[1] it seems to me highly probable that all plays in which we find this peculiar uncertainty as to speech-headings were printed either from the author's original manuscript or from a close transcript of this. I believe that, although Shakespeare generally fixed upon a name for each of his characters at his or her first introduction, in the heat of composition their qualities or the part which they played in the action were often more strongly present to his imagination than their personal names, and that he therefore came instinctively to substitute descriptive titles for their original designations, *Braggart* for *Armado*, *Father* for *Capulet*, and so on, while in other cases he may simply have forgotten whether he had, for example, previously referred to a character as *Princess* or *Queen*.

To follow the original texts in this irregularity would, however, be unnecessarily confusing to a reader, and as, after all, these speech-prefixes are merely labels intended to show to whom the various speeches are to be attributed, it seems to me an editor's clear duty to treat them as labels and to make the labels uniform; to choose, that is, one of the designations given to each character and to prefix this —in the same form and spelling—to every speech of the character throughout the play, except when a change of rank or title necessitates alteration. This is, of course, done in all modernized editions.[2]

It is, however, sometimes difficult to decide which of the two or more names given to a character should be used as the heading of his speeches and I must explain the principle followed. I have, as a rule, provided that there seemed nothing against it, preferred the name which appears in the character's first entry, and in the first speeches assigned to him. Thus, in *Love's Labour's Lost*, the first stage direction has 'Ferdinand K. of Nauar' and the first speech is headed '*Ferdinand*'. I have therefore used *Ferd.* as a speech-prefix throughout, rather than *King*, which was used by Rowe and by most editors since.

So, too, in the same play we find that Costard, Armado, Moth, Holofernes, and Nathaniel all have their personal names at their respective first entries, though actually they are seldom used afterwards,[3] the alternatives, indicating their characteristics or functions

---

[1] See p. 9, n. 1.

[2] A good start on the very useful work of rendering the speech-headings uniform was made by Rowe, in whose first edition of 1709 the majority of the speeches have the prefixes which they retain in modern editions.

[3] For example, in the Quarto of *Love's Labour's Lost* only 6 of Costard's 84

as mentioned above, being much more frequent in what follows. I have therefore used the personal names. Having done this it seemed better to use personal names for the other characters of the sub-plot, namely Anthony Dull and Jaquenetta, in spite of their first appearing as *Constable* and *Wench* (though their names have previously been given in Armado's letter). The use of the personal name, besides probably coming closer to the author's original intention, has the advantage that it fixes the name in the reader's memory and prevents him from being puzzled as to the identity of the persons referred to in the text, as he might otherwise be. In cases where for any reason I have not followed this plan I have given my reasons in the introduction to the play.

At the suggestion of Dr. Alice Walker I have introduced into certain plays a form of speech-heading which seems to me to have great convenience.

In several plays certain of the characters are disguised, and are addressed and referred to by other names than their own. Thus, in *The Taming of the Shrew*, Hortensio feigns to be a music-master and takes the name 'Licio', while Lucentio masquerades as 'Cambio' and Tranio as Lucentio; similarly, in *Love's Labour's Lost*, v. ii. 130–265, the Princess exchanges favours with Rosaline, and Katharine with Maria, in order to trick their suitors. In other plays similar mystifications are to be found. On the stage there is, as a rule, little or no difficulty in penetrating the disguises and following the plot, but to a reader they may be exceedingly troublesome.

I have therefore adopted the device of giving *both* the character's real name and the feigned one; the *real* name, which is the one normally used in modern editions, standing first, while the one which does not appear in the copy-text is within round brackets. Thus the prefix *Hor.* (*Lic.*) means 'Hortensio disguised as Licio' and implies that in the copy-text the name of the character is given as Hortensio. Had the disguise name been used, as was sometimes done,[1] but not in this particular case, the speech-heading would have had the form (*Hor.*) *Lic.*

This method has only been used where characters are disguised as

___

speeches have the heading *Costard*, the remainder having simply *Clown*; while Moth's speeches are never so headed, but 54 are headed *Boy*, and 24 *Page*—the latter form being evidently used to avoid confusion with the *Boy*. which is the regular abbreviation of *Boyet*.

[1] See, for example, *L.L.L.*, v. ii. 242–55.

part of the plot—not in accessory shows such as that of the Nine Worthies in *Love's Labour's Lost*.

Speakers' names repeated after a stage direction. We occasionally find that when a speech is interrupted by an entry or an exit, &c., the name of the speaker is repeated (e.g. *2 Hen. VI*, v. ii. 8, *Rich. III*, III. vii. 58). So far as I have observed, there is no rule as to this. Sometimes the name is repeated, sometimes it is not, and there seems no special significance in the repetition. Presumably it was at the fancy of the writer, who in the original may have written the speech straight on, marking the entry or other action in the margin after he had completed the speech; or alternatively have paused in writing to insert the direction. In the former case he would not, of course, repeat the speaker's name; in the latter he might easily, without thinking, do so. The custom now is, of course, not to repeat, and these repetitions have been eliminated from modern editions. It is obviously less confusing to drop them, as there is then no suggestion of a different speaker, as there may be if they are retained. I therefore have omitted them, but have, of course, noted the fact of their occurrence in the copy-text among the collation notes.

On the other hand, we sometimes find in the early texts that when a character speaks immediately after he has entered alone, his name is not repeated as a speech-prefix, it being evidently regarded as obvious to whom the speech belongs. Thus, in *Richard III*, where we have the heading '*Enter Richard . . . solus*', the opening speech is without prefix in the early texts. Similarly, in *Titus Andronicus*, I. i. 67, Q1 has no speech-prefix for the speech of the captain whose entry has just been recorded.

It should further be noted that in the early texts where we have two or three similar minor characters such as messengers, murderers, citizens, &c., I have attempted to combine clarity with as close an adherence as possible to the speech-prefixes of my copy-text. For example, when a series of messengers enters, the early texts frequently attribute the speeches of the first simply to '*Mess.*'. We may then have the stage direction '*Enter another messenger*', his speech being headed '2. *Mess.*' or simply '*Mess.*', and so on. Modern texts generally call the first to enter '1 *Mess.*', the second and subsequent ones '2 *Mess.*', '3 *Mess.*', &c., regardless of whether they are so numbered in the original or not. There seems no reason at all to differentiate the first as '1 *Mess.*' until there is a second, and not much even then, and I have therefore followed the practice of the copy-text in each case, except, of course, when there is need for distinguishing the speakers; for example, if the first messenger spoke after the second, differentiation would be essential.

LOCALITIES

It is questionable to what extent it is desirable that indications of locality should be added to Shakespearian plays. Some consider, and I believe rightly, that all that is necessary for the appreciation of the play is to be gathered from the text itself and that the assumption of localities not so indicated—especially when these are merely inferred from the sources or from other outside information —is undesirable. In any case indications of locality are not ordinarily to be found in the early editions.[1] I have therefore thought it best to omit indications of locality altogether from the scene-headings of the plays, where they are usually placed.

At the same time it has seemed well to record the accepted localization of the various scenes, and I have therefore, as explained on p. 97, below, given that of the Cambridge editors in the collation notes.

THE NUMBERING OF THE LINES

The lines of the acts and scenes have been numbered on the system which is now usual, but the fact that in some cases I have not followed other editors in assuming that lines printed as prose were intended to be verse will, of course, at times make the numbering differ considerably from theirs.

It appeared to me that for the purposes of general reference it would be convenient if the lines of each play were numbered throughout, as is done, for example, in the plays issued by the Malone Society and in many other modern editions of plays. It is an obvious advantage to be able to refer to a particular line as '*1 Hen. VI*, 2240' instead of '*1 Hen. VI*, IV. vii. 10'. On the other hand, such a consecutive numbering cannot be based on the lines as printed in a *modern* edition, for obviously editions are likely to vary to an extent which will completely upset the correspondence after the first hundred lines

---

[1] Exceptions are 'An vn-inhabited Island' as the scene of *The Tempest*, and '*Vienna*' as that of *Measure for Measure*. A few incidental indications are also found in the stage directions as in *1 Hen. VI*, IV. ii, where Talbot appears '*with Trumpe and Drumme, before Burdeaux*', and *Rich. III*, III. iii, where Sir Richard Ratcliff enters '*carrying the Nobles to death at Pomfret*'.

or so. If, however, we take the typographical lines of the First Folio as our standard and print opposite to every tenth line of our text the number of the line of the First Folio, we shall get a numbering of the lines which can be used by any other editor or commentator and may reasonably be regarded as permanent. I have therefore in this edition not only numbered the lines of text in the customary manner within the scenes, but have inserted as well, in italic type and within square brackets, the number of every tenth line of the Folio. It is true that there are certain obvious difficulties. In prose passages the number given may not be the number of the whole line in the Folio, but of only part of it, for ten lines of our text may correspond to twelve in the Folio. In using the numbers we must therefore always admit a possible error of one or two lines in the prose. On the other hand, where a verse line of my text which should properly be numbered does not correspond exactly to a typographical line of the Folio, owing either to a turnover, to the line being differently divided, or to the different placing of a stage direction, the number is attached to the nearest line which *exactly* corresponds to a line of the Folio. Thus, for example, in *1 Henry VI*, line 310 of the Folio consists merely of the turnover ('weake.') of the speech which appears in my text (I. ii. 106) as a single line: viz.

Pucel. Christs Mother helpes me, else I were too weake.

As the line of my text thus contains not only F310 but also F309, I do not number this line but insert opposite I. ii. 107, which contains neither more nor less than the corresponding line of the Folio, the number [*311*].

Further, in certain plays, such as *Richard III* and *Lear*, there is a special difficulty owing to the fact that the text printed contains certain lines which are absent from the Folio and have been here inserted, following general editorial opinion, from Quartos. In such cases the inserted lines are numbered from 1 onwards, a small plus sign being affixed to the number. Thus in *Richard III*, IV. ii. 99, line *2696* of the continuous numbering is followed by a passage of 20 lines not found in the Folio texts. These are numbered *1* to *20* and should be referred to as [*2696+1*], [*2696+2*], and so on. This method has the advantage of calling attention to the insertion of lines which are not in the Folio. It must, however, be noted that *portions* of lines not in the Folio have no special numbering.

In the very rare case of it being necessary to *omit* a line which is given by the Folio, the number of the line is given in the collation notes where the line is quoted.

It will not, of course, be possible to ascertain the numbering of every line in the Folio by reference to my text. On the other hand if, as is to be hoped, an edition of the Folio with numbered lines is produced in the near future it will be possible to refer from it, or anything using its numeration, to this text. Further, the numbering makes it possible for me, in the notes and introductions, to refer to plays not yet in print in this edition.

III

THE RECORDING OF THE READINGS OF OTHER
EDITIONS THAN THE COPY-TEXT

IT has been my endeavour not only to present the text of Shakespeare in a form which, in view of the evidence which has come
down to us, approaches as nearly as possible to what we may suppose
a fair copy of his works made by himself would have been, but also,
whenever there seemed any reason to doubt the soundness of a reading of the edition in each case chosen as copy-text, to put the reader
in a position to form his own judgement by recording the readings of
certain other selected editions.

On pp. 10–18, 36–8, above, I have explained the principles by which
I think that we must be guided in the selection of an edition to follow
as copy-text in each case, and have said something in general of the
use that other editions may be, whether or not they appear to have
any independent authority, in supporting or emending readings in
the copy-text which, for various reasons, seem of doubtful authenti-
city. It is, however, necessary to consider somewhat further the
extent of the collation of variant readings which can be usefully
attempted and the editions to be collated.

Before we do this, however, we must be quite clear as to what
constitutes a variant reading, for many editors appear to confuse
genuine variants with those substituted forms and spellings which
would at all periods normally be found in any reprinted book intended
for any but an antiquarian public.

MODERNIZATION AND VARIATION

It is not, I think, always recognized that with very few exceptions,
and these deliberate ones, *all* editions of Shakespeare until quite
recent times have been modernized editions. Every reprint[1] from the
very earliest has, to the best of the printer's ability, eliminated antiquated spellings and followed the typographical practice of its own
day. This is true no less of the First Folio than of Rowe's or Pope's
or the Cambridge edition. Indeed, the only essential difference in

---

[1] Indeed we might, I think, include the original editions, in which we may
assume that the printer often followed his own practice with regard to orthography,
as was indeed the general custom of his time.

the practice of the various press readers or editors has been that in certain cases when a word had greatly altered its current form recent editors have restored the older one, though spelling it in a modern way. But such modernization as occurs in the transmission of a text must be carefully distinguished from variation, and as editors do not seem always to have been quite clear as to the distinction I must be pardoned for devoting a few words to the subject.

There are two entirely different purposes for which we may wish to know the readings of editions of our author other than the one which we are following as the main source of our own text. On the one hand, we may wish to know whether such editions have the same reading as our copy-text or substitute another, in order that we may better judge whether our reading is correct or whether an alternative reading exists or an acceptable emendation has been proposed. On the other hand, we may wish to know the readings of *later* texts, derived from our copy-texts, in order to see how the editors of such texts understood the reading in the one before us.

In the first case there is, or may be, a question of a variant reading, the point being whether the copy-text is correct or no: in the second, the correctness of the copy-text is not in question; we wish merely for help in interpreting it.[1] It appears to me that the massing together of readings which are required for these two distinct purposes in one set of collation notes can only lead to confusion and to a misunderstanding of the real problems of textual criticism.

In this edition therefore the collation notes will be concerned only with what are properly variant readings. Any readings which it is thought desirable to quote from later editions in order to show how the editors of these interpreted what they found in their copy-texts will be given in the explanatory notes, where all other questions of meaning are dealt with.

For our purpose, then, 'variant readings' as between a later edition and an earlier one on the same line of descent may be defined as not merely readings which differ from one another, but readings the later of which cannot have been derived from the earlier by the normal

---

[1] Thus, on the one hand, we may suspect that the famous 'Table of greene fields' in *Hen. V*, II. iii (F839), is an error, and wish to know whether and how the various editors have emended it. On the other hand, we may have in our text the word 'and' so placed that it might be equivalent either to present-day 'and' or to 'if', and we may wish to know whether the modern editors had retained 'and' or had shown, by spelling the word 'an', that they understood it in the latter sense.

process of modernization: or, to put the matter in another way, a reading in a later edition can only be considered as a 'variant' in respect of an earlier reading if it implies an attempt to emend that reading.

Thus, if an early text has the spelling 'mushrump' and a later one on the same line of descent has 'mushroom', the latter would not be regarded as a variant (and consequently would not be recorded in the collations), as it is simply the normal form which, in a text intended to be modernized (i.e. brought into accordance with the spelling of its day), would necessarily replace the earlier one.[1]

So, too, if an early text has the word 'trauaile', a modern text having either 'travel' or 'travail' (as the case required) would not be regarded as varying from it, because either of the modern spellings would imply the same *word* (whether spelt 'trauaile' or 'trauel') in the early text; or, to put it in another way, neither spelling in the modern text could be regarded as implying correction or alteration of the early one. If therefore it is desired, for the purpose of elucidating the text, to indicate how the modern text has interpreted the original ambiguous spelling, whether, that is, the word is printed 'travel' or 'travail', the proper place for the statement of this will be in an *explanatory note*, not among the collations, which are only concerned with variants.

It must be noted that this practice is quite contrary to that of the Cambridge editors, and many others, who have proceeded on the rule that if two readings found in texts collated suggest different words *in modern spelling* they must be treated as variants and recorded in the collations.

Thus 'heard' (*audivit*) might in the sixteenth century be spelt 'heard', herd', or 'hard', while 'heart' (*cor*) might also be spelt 'hart'. Because there happen to be modern English words 'herd', 'hard', and 'hart', such editors treat those spellings not merely as alternative spellings of 'heard' and 'heart' but as variants, and record them. On the other hand, the word 'beard' might be spelt also as 'berd' or 'bard', but 'berd', not being a modern word, would not be regarded as a variant, though 'bard' would.

In a similar way collations on this system distinguish between

[1] On the other hand, 'mushrump' and 'mushroom' might be regarded as variants when they occur in two substantive texts. Whether one would so regard them would depend on the detail into which one was going as regards the differences, and the purpose of the collation.

'practice' and 'practise', 'deuice' and 'deuise', and so on, merely because these are *now* different words and not merely alternative spellings as they formerly were.

The rule is certainly simple and saves trouble in deciding what to include in the collations and what to omit, but it is utterly illogical, for from the sixteenth-century point of view there is no more reason to distinguish between 'hard' and 'herd' as variant spellings of 'heard' than between 'freend', 'frind', and 'freind' as variant spellings of 'friend'. If, then, *these* spellings are not recorded in the collations, there can be no justification whatever for recording the others. It may of course sometimes happen—though indeed rarely—that the question should arise how one of these forms should be understood, whether, for example, 'hard' is to be interpreted as the modern 'heard' or 'hard', and it might even be necessary to give the actual forms used in the early texts, but the proper place for such discussion would be in the explanatory notes, not in the collations.

Among forms which are therefore here not treated as variants nor recorded in the collations may be mentioned the following. There are many others but these will be sufficient as examples:

breath, breathe; clime, climb; deuice, deuise; heard, hard, herd; heart, hart; loose, lose; looser, loser; practice, practise; precedent, president; reuerend, reuerent; right, rite; sight, site; waits, weights.

Nor are such forms as 'murther', 'lanthorn', varying with 'murder', 'lantern', noticed. There seems no more reason for treating these as variants than for recording the variation of 'dance', 'daunce', &c., though many editors have done this.

I have, of course, treated place and personal names in a similar manner. When there is any likelihood that the reader may require a gloss on names found in the text or stage directions I have included one among the *explanatory* notes. There is, of course, no more reason for recording among the collation notes the later spellings of, say, 'Ouergne' (i.e. Auvergne) or 'Burgonie' (i.e. Burgundy) than there is for recording the later spellings of 'murther' or 'lanthorn'.

Having thus, I hope, cleared the ground by explaining what I regard as a variant reading, and what I do not so regard, I will now consider what variants are to be recorded, and the form which the collations are to take.

In the first place it is obvious that all that is found in the copy-text must be recorded somewhere. All rejected readings of this must therefore be included in the collation notes.[1]

Secondly, if we conclude that an edition descended from the copy-text has no independent authority, its readings can have no claim whatever to be included on their own account. Whenever, then, the copy-text supplies a reading, the soundness of which there seems no reason to doubt, the readings of the later editions[2] are as a general rule ignored except that, for the reasons given on pp. 70–1, I have thought it necessary to record the readings of the First Folio in the case of plays printed from a Quarto. This in its turn has rendered it necessary in some cases to record the readings of the Quarto or Quartos intermediate between the copy-text and the First Folio, as these sometimes explain the reading of the latter. On the other hand, when the readings of F1 agree with those of the copy-text I have, as a rule, thought it unnecessary to record intermediate variants.

It should further be noted that I do not record obvious misprints in the First Folio when this is not being used as copy-text, except in a few cases where the misprint gave rise to a reading which is found in a number of later editions.

When, however, the reading of the copy-text appears to be erroneous or doubtful and the readings of later texts are, or appear to be, attempts to emend it, such of these later readings as seem of value are given.

It is, however, to be remembered that this edition is solely an attempt to present the Shakespearian text as nearly as possible, having regard to the material which has come down to us, in the form in which its author or those persons who revised his manuscripts left it, and that it is no part of my purpose to record the history of editorial opinion or practice as regards that text, which would be a very different thing. I have therefore made no attempt whatever in the collation notes to put readers in the position of being able to reconstruct from them the later texts, but have kept before me merely the question of how these later editions corrected or interpreted the copy-text.

[1] An exception is made in the case of simple misprints in speakers' names when there is no doubt who is intended. As these are in any case normalized (see p. 57) there seems no purpose in recording such a meaningless error as *Clew.* for *Clow.* (i.e. *Clown*). Further, when necessary punctuation is supplied at the end of a speech in accordance with the practice described on p. 40, n. 1, collations are not given.

[2] Of such are, for example, the great majority of the attempts to tinker with grammar and metre found in F2.

In this connexion it must be understood that, as the readings of other texts are not given for their own sakes, but merely as supporting, or as failing to support, the reading of my text, no greater degree of exactitude in presenting them has been aimed at than seemed necessary for this purpose. To give all readings noted exactly in the form in which they occur in the editions from which they are cited would have enormously, and for my purpose uselessly, extended the collation notes. I will return to this point later.

Further, in many cases where the text appears to be corrupt, a great number of emendations have been proposed, some of which have no merit whatever except that they make sense, while others can hardly be said even to do that. There are, it must be admitted, many lines in the original editions which it is impossible to believe to be as Shakespeare left them, or meant to leave them, and many of these—especially those which are metrically defective—can be emended in a great number of ways all equally possible. In such cases the earlier editors, especially Pope, generally introduced one or other of the possible emendations—often expanding or contracting verbal forms, e.g. 'blessed' or 'blest', or introducing slurred forms such as 'dang'rous', 'int'rest', as might be required; while later editors have commonly left the text as it stood, though sometimes mentioning the proposed emendations. I have generally not thought it worth while to record these, or at most have only mentioned such as struck me as unusually happy, for there seems to be little use in recording, as that of a particular editor, the kind of guess which would naturally occur to any reader of normal intelligence, especially when that guess is only one of several, all of which, so far as one can tell, are equally likely to be correct.

It may here be noted that the eighteenth-century editors made a practice of regularly using an apostrophe to indicate a slurred syllable, writing for example 'Ev'n' for 'Even' and 'tow'rd' for 'toward' when these are to be spoken as monosyllables. In the same way they have 'monast'ry', 'marv'lous', 'heav'n', 'pray'r', 'Marg'ret', 'length'ned', 'desp'rate', 'ling'ring', and so on. They also make use of the apostrophe in such spellings as 'altho'' and in ''Would that' (for 'I would that'). All such tinkerings may be properly regarded as modernizations and I have in general ignored them in the collations. Similarly, I have in general ignored the variations between 'long' and 'short' spellings already referred to on p. 24 and the attempts of some editors to indicate the number of syllables required in words such as 'Rouen' or 'fire' by the use of diaeresis or other devices.

THE EDITIONS COLLATED

It is of course to be understood that I have made no attempt to take account of all the editions of Shakespeare or even to record all the emendations that have been proposed of difficult passages. To do this efficiently would, I suppose, be the work of a considerable body of people over a long period of years, and it seems likely that the result of such an endeavour would be so complicated as to be entirely useless. It appears to me that the texts which are important are:

1. The early Quartos and the First Folio, which alone can be of *authority* in the establishment of the text.
2. The later Folios[1] and the early 'edited' editions, in particular those of Rowe, Pope, Theobald, Johnson, Capell, and Malone, in which the text was freed from a number of careless irregularities of transmission and ordered and interpreted from what we may call a common-sense point of view.
3. Certain modern editions, beginning with the Cambridge edition of 1863–6, in which the results of previous work are reconsidered and crystallized.

While there are other editions which must be taken into consideration for particular points, it seems to me that ninety-nine hundredths of all that matters is to be found in one of these groups.

As regards group 1, the early editions, it is probable that in most cases there is only one text, that which has been selected as copy-text, which really contains anything of authority, all variants from this being merely errors or pure conjectures. If one could be certain of this it would, of course, so long as the readings of the copy-text appear sound, be useless to give the readings of any other

---

[1] I have recorded the readings of the later Folios more because it is customary and on the whole convenient to do so than because of any conviction of their value. It was long ago shown by Malone, in the preface to his edition of 1790, pp. xx–xlii, that as a whole the alterations of the Second Folio were valueless. They are, in fact, mere attempts to bring Shakespeare's language more or less up to date, by getting rid of certain locutions which were quite normal in his day, but which had passed out of use by 1632, and by 'correction' of grammar when this appeared to the editor to be faulty. The Fourth Folio seems to have been fairly carefully read with a view to regularizing the punctuation, but there is nothing more in this than we should expect from an ordinary corrector of the press.

editions at all. Unfortunately, however, we cannot be quite certain of it.[1] Some Quartos may contain readings derived from persons, actors or others, who had a recollection of the performances, or from copies of previous editions corrected by such persons. In the introduction to each play of which there are Quartos I have discussed the possible authority of these and have stated to what extent I have attempted to collate them.

In particular it appears to me that we must pay especial attention to the readings of the First Folio. In the case of certain plays it is at least possible that the text was printed from a copy of an earlier Quarto which had been used in the theatre as a prompt copy,[2] and in which certain stage directions useful to a prompter had been added. But if this were done by the prompter it is equally possible that he would correct in this copy any serious errors of the text which he noticed and which might prove troublesome to him when prompting. He might indeed correct them by guess-work, but he might also correct them from his or an actor's knowledge of the play, and if Shakespeare himself supervised the early performances and corrected the actors, an alteration made by the prompter in the copy used by him might ultimately be derived from the author. The possibility of this, however remote it may be, means that we must give the apparent corrections of text found in the Folio, and once we begin to give variants it is impossible to stop short of giving a complete collation— except of course for obvious textual misprints.[3]

The case is perhaps less strong for giving a full collation of the First Folio in the plays where there is no evidence of printing from a Quarto used in the theatre, but even here we have evidence of the use of occasional care in preparation of the text, and there is therefore some probability of an attempt being made to correct in all cases in which, to the editor, the text appeared to be erroneous. This being so, as I have already suggested on p. 38, above, the leaving in the First Folio of a passage untouched which appears to us to be erroneous is of some value as evidence that it may be correct and our failure to

---

[1] See pp. 16–17.

[2] See, for example, the introduction to *Titus Andronicus*, the Folio edition of which seems to have been printed from a copy in which certain incidental music had been noted.

[3] This, of course, is not to be construed as implying any particular and consistent merits in the First Folio as a piece of editing. Whatever was done to it by the persons in charge of the volume seems to have been to a great extent haphazard.

understand it be due to our loss of some allusion which was familiar at the time.[1]

On these grounds it has seemed to me necessary in the case of plays printed from a Quarto to record in all cases the reading of the Folio, though in accordance with the principles of the edition I have been as sparing as possible in introducing such readings into the text.

In regard to group 2, the question may well be asked: What do Rowe, Pope, and the rest of the eighteenth-century editors matter to us? Can we not ignore them and start afresh? After all, their view of textual problems was very different from ours and their contribution to Shakespearian scholarship consisted mainly of guesses. At first sight such a view is attractive. It would certainly save an editor a world of trouble if he could simply print the most authoritative of the early texts with such emendations as seemed to him necessary. I had indeed some such idea myself when I began this work, but I soon came to the conclusion that an edition which proceeded on these lines, even if it were possible, would be very unsatisfactory.

In the first place an editor's work necessarily involves interpretation, and a conscientious editor not only must feel reluctance in claiming as his own an interpretation (sometimes not very obvious) that he owes to his predecessors, but at the same time must, in doubtful cases, wish for their support. These eighteenth-century editors did indeed expect from Shakespeare, and attempt to impose upon him, a certain smoothness of rhythm and an attention to what they regarded as grammatical propriety, which we now recognize as not belonging to his period, but this, as well as their ignorance of certain forms of language which were current in his day but not in theirs, we can easily discount. On the other hand, they were by no means fools, and they were nearer to his day, and nearer especially to the stage for which he wrote, than we are. Rowe was a practised dramatist. Pope, for all the occasional obtuseness of which Theobald makes so much, and a kind of impatience with what seemed to him inferior stuff that was not worth bothering about, was keenly appreciative of all that was excellent either as poetry or as drama. Theobald, who read, as he tells us, 700 plays for the purpose of his edition, and who had the advantage which few of the later generations of scholars have

[1] It should be clearly understood that the altering or leaving unaltered of a passage in F1 is only evidence that the editor thought that the text was wrong or right; it does not follow that he was correct in his belief, nor that any alteration made by him actually restored the author's words.

had of reading all these in the original editions and not in modernized reprints, while not, I think, quite so careful or conscientious as he made himself out to be, was a person of great ingenuity as well as common sense; and he also, if not a successful dramatist like Rowe, had written for the stage within a century of Shakespeare's death, and a stage which—if theatrical customs were as slow to change as they have been in more recent times—probably retained much of the tradition of the Jacobean period. To ignore the interpretation which these earlier editors placed on the many doubtful passages of Shakespearian text would, it seems to me, not only be a wrong to the pioneers in our study, but be a material loss to ourselves. To give in such cases the readings of Rowe, Pope, and the others must not then be taken to imply an interest in the eighteenth-century point of view for its own sake— or that an editor is trying to give a picture of Shakespeare through the ages:[1] it implies as a rule merely an admission that he regards the text as probably wrong, or at least doubtful, and that he thinks it helpful to the modern reader to be told how certain persons of intelligence and ingenuity, who were nearer to Shakespeare in point of time than we are, interpreted it, and when they had, in their view, a choice of readings of equal authority, which they chose.[2]

The editions belonging to this group which have been generally collated for the present edition are the following: Rowe 1709,[3] Pope 1723-5, Theobald 1733, Johnson 1765, Capell 1768, Malone 1790, Cambridge 1863-6.[4] In addition to this, in the case of the majority of the plays one or more recent editions have been collated. These are mentioned in the introductions to the several plays.[5]

[1] For *that* purpose it would be far more important to give the alterations made by the editors where the text is *not* in doubt.

[2] In a few cases, however, readings for which there can be in my view no real authority have been recorded in collations because they have been admitted into texts regarded as important and may be regarded as having become part of the vulgate Shakespeare, e.g. Theobald's 'Lady-love' in *R. & J.*, i. ii. 95.

[3] The reprint of, probably, 1710 (Rowe ii) and the duodecimo edition of 1714 (Rowe iii) have also been consulted, and 'Rowe' alone implies in the collation the agreement of all three. It should be remarked that the edition called here Rowe ii was not distinguished until recently from Rowe i. See my letter in *The Times Literary Supplement*, 8 March 1934.

[4] I have actually worked with the Cambridge text of 1891-3, but so far as everything but the correction of a very few misprints and the addition of collations of some later editions is concerned the two Cambridge editions are almost identical.

[5] As a rule the volumes of the (English) Arden edition have been collated. The amount of attention given to the text by the various editors differs, however, greatly, and in some cases I have not regarded a full collation as worth while.

Further, for particular points, a number of other editions have been collated such as Rowe's second and third editions, [1710] and 1714, Theobald's second edition, 1740, and those of Hanmer 1743-4, Warburton 1747, Steevens 1773, 1778, 1793, the three 'Variorum' editions of 1803, 1813, and 1821, Dyce's third edition, 1874, the 'Furness Variorum' and the 'New Shakespeare' of Quiller-Couch and Dover Wilson, as well as several others, but the agreement of these with the editions mentioned above is never to be inferred unless this is specifically stated.[1] The readings of such editions other than those 'generally collated' have, as a rule, only been recorded

(1) when a particular reading which has obtained the approval of some of the editors of the 'generally collated' editions has originated in one of these editions;

(2) in a few particularly difficult or notable passages in which it seems interesting to have a record of the readings of as many as possible of the important editions.

It may be found that there is some irregularity in the use of the editions above mentioned, the number of readings given from some of them, e.g. those of Steevens, being greater in some plays than in others. This is due to two principal causes. On the one hand, almost all editors seem to have had favourite plays on the text of which they expended more work than on that of others; and, on the other, in some plays of which there exist Quarto texts the mass of collations became so great that I thought it better to cut down the number of later editions cited which merely repeated earlier readings.

THE FORM OF THE COLLATION

In the case of the collation of, say, the extant manuscripts of a poetical work, all written at about the same period, the comparison of the readings is, as a rule, a simple matter. One has merely to carry down as a lemma the word in question as it stands in the manuscript which is used as copy-text and add, with the appropriate sigla, the variants of the other manuscripts in some such form as the following,

melde] molde BC

—by which it will be understood that the manuscript used as the

---

[1] As, however, the descent of the text was Rowe i > Rowe ii > Rowe iii > Pope i > Pope ii > Theo. i > Theo. ii > Warburton > Johnson, it normally happens that a reading found in Rowe i and Johnson will be found in all the intermediate editions. This is, however, not the case with Hanmer's edition, which contains a number of readings peculiar to itself.

copy-text agrees with all the other known manuscripts except B and C in reading 'melde', and that B and C read 'molde'.

This is simple, and it might seem that an editor of Shakespeare ought in his collation to follow a similar method, but in practice this would be impossible. In the first place the number of editions of Shakespeare is, as I have said, far too large for any one man, or even any reasonable-sized committee, to be able to collate, while even if the number of those collated is restricted to some half-dozen of the more important, the fact of these having been produced at periods varying over three centuries and, for the most part, following the spelling and typographical practice of their own period complicates the matter in an extraordinary degree. Furthermore, whatever particular list of editions one may choose for *general* collation, it will often be necessary to record readings or conjectures of interest occurring in others, while at the same time it will *not* be necessary to record certain obviously absurd or erroneous readings of the selected list. In many cases fuller knowledge of Elizabethan language or phraseology has enabled us to dismiss as impossible the conjectures of the eighteenth-century editors, such as Pope, and there can be no point in recording what is undoubtedly wrong. It is therefore necessary to stipulate that the giving of a variant as that of a particular edition *must not be taken to imply that the readings of all other editions, or even of those generally collated, agree with that printed in the text.* Thus, such a note as

man] one Theo.

must not be taken to mean more than it says, i.e. that for the word 'man' Theobald here prints 'one'. The passage may have been emended by other editors in a dozen different ways, but the only emendation which it has seemed to me worth recording is that of Theobald.

This system makes it necessary to use a form of collation note which may seem objectionable to some, though it has been the practice of Shakespearian editors at any rate since the Cambridge edition of 1863–6, i.e. to print, for example, as a note to a text based on F1,

matter] F1, Camb.: matters F2–Mal.[1]

[1] In order to keep my collation notes as brief as possible I have regularly abbreviated the longer sigla of the editions normally collated, using Theo., Johns., Cap., Mal., Camb. for the editions of Theobald, Johnson, Capell, Malone, and the Cambridge editors respectively. In cases where the (English) Arden edition or the New Cambridge Shakespeare has been regularly collated I have used similar

As I am in this case using F1 as the copy-text, it may seem un-necessary to record that its reading is the one adopted. On the other hand, to give simply

matter] matters F2–Mal.

would not do, because, though I normally collate the Cambridge text, I have stated that the agreement of uncited texts with mine must *not* be inferred from their non-citation; and therefore there would be no means of knowing in this case what the reading of the Cambridge text is. Nor would

matter] **Camb.**: matters F2–Mal.

do, as this would give the impression that the reading was an emendation due to the Cambridge editors, unless and until the reader took the trouble to discover that F1 was not cited. He might do this and might consequently infer that F1 must have the reading printed in the text: but it is much simpler, and safer, in such cases to in-sert F1.

Two points should be noted as regards the form of the collations.

1. *Lemmas.* I regard a lemma as merely serving to identify the word or passage in the text to which the variant reading corresponds, and it seems to me therefore unnecessary to occupy space by giving a lemma when there can be no doubt as to the text-reading referred to. Thus when it is merely necessary to record the existence in the copy-text of a simple misprint I usually give this without a lemma; e.g. if a word which should evidently be 'whose' is printed in the copy-text as 'wohse' I merely give a note in the form

wohse Q1

Similarly, when I wish to record an obvious error of puctuation in the copy-text, such as, for example, a full stop where a query is called for, I print such a collation as

state. Q1–4

not as

state?] Q5+: state. Q1–4[1]

Wherever there can possibly be any ambiguity as to the word to which the collation refers, I have, however, always given a lemma.

abbreviations of the names of their editors. The symbol '–', as explained below, p. 86, is used to indicate the agreement of editions normally collated between those specifically mentioned. The colon is, of course, used to separate one variant and its siglum or sigla from another.

[1] The plus sign indicates the agreement of later editions collated. See below, pp. 80–1.

2. *Punctuation belonging to collated words.* When the reading of a word or phrase varies I ordinarily give the readings of that word or phrase *alone*, without any *final* punctuation, unless that punctuation is a significant part of the variation, though I give of course intermediate punctuation in the lemma and the variants cited. Thus if one text had 'Ha, ha,' and another simply 'Ha,' the final comma would be omitted and the collation would take the form

Ha, ha] F1+: Ha Qq

Further, the collation would be the same if the texts read respectively 'Ha, ha,' and 'Ha' (without a comma) unless the absence of the comma in the second case was regarded as having significance.

Suppose, however, that in one or other case the absence of a comma might suggest that the words bore or could bear a different interpretation; if, for example, one had the two readings

Ha, ha ye men who will follow me?

and

Ha, ye men who will follow me?

it is evident that the first line *may* mean 'Ha! have ye men who will follow me?' The punctuation of 'Ha, ha' and 'Ha,' becomes therefore significant and the note would take the form

Ha, ha∧] F1+: Ha, Qq

the caret being used to draw attention to the absence of punctuation after the second 'ha' in F1+.

Thus if final punctuation is given either in the lemma or in any reading cited, the final punctuation of *all* readings is given, or if in any particular case there is none, its absence is indicated by a caret.

Evidently when we quote a complete phrase which is omitted in a certain text and which has its own final punctuation we must include this in citing the phrase. Thus in *Richard II*, IV. i. 302–4, Q4 has

Ile begge one boone,
And then be gone, and trouble you no more.

while F1 has

Ile begge one Boone,
And then be gone, and trouble you no more.
Shall I obtaine it?

As I print the last half-line, the question-mark must be included in the lemma, thus

Shall . . . it?] F1+: *om.* Q4, 5

In the same way, when there is a question of the addition or

omission of a whole stage direction the final stop of the direction
will necessarily be a part of the collation; e.g.

Exit Greene.] F1+: *om.* Qq

On the other hand, if one direction had '*Exit Greene.*' and the other,
that of my text, '*Exit Greene and Bushy.*', the collation would be

and Bushy] F1+: *om.* Qq

Further, in giving collations I make use of certain conventions, and
I may say here that the conventions, which at first sight may appear
somewhat complicated and even perverse, have only been adopted
after careful thought and experiment, and actually do—at least in my
deliberate opinion—make it possible to give all necessary facts in the
minimum of space.

1. No regard is paid to differences of spelling, capitalization, &c.
Thus, suppose that in a certain line F1 has 'seruante', F2 'servante',
F3 'servant', F4 'Servant', while Rowe has 'Servants' and all later
editors have 'servants', the plural form being evidently correct: in
such a case I ignore all the varieties of spelling, treating the readings
of F2–4 as equivalent to that of F1, namely 'seruante', and those of all
the later editions as equivalent to Rowe's 'Servants'. Further, as the
only point at issue is whether the word is singular or plural, and as
I always preserve in my text as much as possible of the word as it
appears in the copy-text from which I print, making only such alteration as I suppose that a contemporary corrector would have made,
I keep the final e of 'seruante' in F1 and simply add an s, not
replacing the word by 'Servants' as Rowe has it. Nevertheless, my
collation note will read

seruantes] **Rowe+**: seruante **Ff**

This means, *not* that Rowe actually has the form 'seruantes', but
merely that I take the emendation of the word from singular to plural
from Rowe. As it may safely be assumed that Rowe would have
printed the word in the form usual at his time, there seems no possible
value in giving his actual reading, and printing

seruantes] Servants **Rowe+**: seruante **Ff**

—to say nothing of the fact that if one is at pains to record the actual
spelling of Rowe's text, it seems illogical not equally to record that
Pope and later editors spell 'servants' with a small s, and that the four
Folios all spell the word differently.

It must therefore be understood that a siglum *following a lemma* indicates only that the reading of the text which the lemma represents is *supported by* the text of which it is the siglum, and not (*unless the siglum is that of the copy-text*) that it is in spelling or typographical form identical with it; and further, as regards other readings recorded, that it is only the *first* edition to which a reading is attributed that necessarily has the reading in exactly the form cited; the others may, and generally do, vary from it in accordance with the orthography and typographical practice which they happen to follow.[1] This is in accordance with the principle already explained on p. 77. Thus, to give one further example:

Face] Ff: Faces **Rowe**+

Here the plus sign would indicate only that Pope, Theobald, Johnson, Capell, and the rest of the editions normally collated had the plural, not that they spelt it with a capital, for none of these editions ordinarily capitalizes nouns, though Rowe does, and they must be understood to follow their ordinary practice. If for any reason the question of whether the word had a capital or not were of importance the point would, of course, be specifically noticed.

In this connexion the following points should be noticed as regards the use of i, j, u, and v in the text type of the Folios.

The First Folio follows the sixteenth-century convention, spelling

ioy, iniunction, loue, vse.

The Second and later Folios follow the modern convention and have

joy, injunction, love, use.

As regards capitals, the first two Folios have only I and V, both in roman and italics.[2]

The Third Folio has the full modern use of I, J, U, and V in roman, printing

Joyn, Unlesse, &c.

and generally in italics as

Jack Cade, Ulysses,

though occasionally, perhaps owing to a shortage of type, we find *Vlysses*.

---

[1] Thus 'as well', 'as soon', 'shall be', &c., are regarded simply as modern spellings of 'aswel', 'assone', 'shalbe', &c.

[2] The swash italic *J* seems curiously rare in these Folios, but if it was employed at all it would certainly not have been distinguished in use from the plain form.

Thus where the First Folio has 'liue', the Second, intending the same reading, would have 'live', and these must be treated as identical. Not only do I therefore give collations such as

saue Ff

when actually the readings of F2-4 are 'save', but supposing, for example, that in a certain passage F1 and F2 had 'fine', whereas F3 and F4 had 'five' and the latter was obviously correct, I should print in the text 'fiue', and not 'five', both because this is how it would have been spelt in the copy-text if the compositor had not chanced to misread his manuscript, and because the misreading is a much more intelligible one if it is remembered that it is a case of n for u, not n for v. It would be possible in such a case to give a collation note in the form

fiue] fine F1, 2: five F3, 4

This would be correct, but misleading, for it conceals the fact that the reading adopted is actually that of F3.

Further, supposing that the facts had been reversed, F1, 2 having an incorrect 'fiue' and 'five', F3 and F4 a correct 'fine', the natural way of giving the collation would be

fine] F3, 4: fiue F1, 2

It therefore appears to be logical to give the collation in the first case as

fiue] F3, 4: fine F1, 2

in spite of the fact that the actual reading of F3 is 'five'.

Similarly, supposing that F1 had 'deuide', F2-4 'devide', Rowe 'divide', and that Pope had altered the word to 'divine' with universal acceptance: I should in this case print 'deuine', the form which I suppose F1 to have intended, with the note

deuine] Pope+: deuide F1-Rowe

and expect it to be understood that Pope and Rowe had really given the words indicated in the form customary at their dates, i.e. respectively 'divine' and 'divide'.

2. A second convention is that in giving readings I ignore misprints[1] in any edition after the first cited. Thus, supposing that in the

---

[1] Provided that there is no doubt that they *are* misprints. When what is probably a misprint happens to form a word, I generally regard it as safer to record it as in the case mentioned on p. 82, below. See also the reservations on p. 67, above. It should be noted that attempts in later editions to *emend* misprints in editions other than

'servant' readings cited above, the Third Folio instead of 'servant' had 'sevrant', I should take no notice of the error and treat it exactly as if it had read 'servant', as it was clearly intended that it should.

3. A third convention is that when readings of two texts are *in intention* the same though actually they differ slightly, I treat them as the same. Thus, suppose the Folios to read 'poyson'd', and Theobald to read 'prison'd', in which he is followed by all later editors except one who chooses to read 'pris'n'd'. This last reading is evidently intended to differ from Theobald's in being monosyllabic instead of disyllabic, but a difference of this kind alone would not, according to the practice of this edition, necessitate the giving of a collation at all (see p. 68). The point of the collation in this case is whether the reading is essentially 'prisoned' or 'poisoned', and so far as this is concerned the readings of Theobald and all later editors are identical. I should therefore give a collation in the form

poyson'd] F1–Pope: prison'd Theo.+

Perhaps I should add as a fourth convention that readers of the book are expected to use ordinary common sense in interpreting the collations. For example in *Richard III*, IV. iv. 30, the reading of the Folios is 'innocent blood', that of the Quartos 'innocents bloud' (*or* 'blood'). I give the collation

30 innocent] F1±: innocents Qq, Camb.[1]

By this I mean it to be understood that the Cambridge text has, in accordance with modern usage, 'innocents' blood'—for the sense can of course only be 'the blood of innocents'. It seems to me quite unnecessary, and indeed contrary to my general rule (see p. 26), to make 'innocents' blood' into a separate reading, seeing that this is evidently what is intended by the Quartos.

SPECIAL SYMBOLS

The following special symbols have been used in giving the collations:

+ after the siglum of any edition implies the agreement of all editions 'generally collated' (see pp. 69–72) which are subsequent to

---

the copy-text are similarly ignored, except when they provide an explanation of a reading which was long accepted as a genuine variant.

[1] For the plus-minus sign see p. 81, below. The siglum Qq refers in each case to the Quartos collated for each particular play; these are normally only those which appeared not later than F1, i.e. in or before 1622.

the one cited, together with any editions specially mentioned as collated in the introduction to the particular play. Besides saving much space, this sign has the advantage of calling attention to the generally accepted reading in cases where there is one.

The plus sign, however, is attached only to editions in the same line of descent. Thus in the collation notes to *Titus Andronicus*, where there is only one substantive text, namely Q1, the siglum Q1+ would include the Quartos, the Folios, and all subsequent editions generally collated. In the collation notes to *Richard III*, on the other hand, where the Folio text does not apparently derive as a whole from the Quarto, so that there are two substantive texts, Q1 and F1, a reading occurring in the Quartos, the Folios, and subsequent texts would have the sigla Qq, F1+, not Q1+, unless this happened to occur in those parts of the play where Q1 was the only substantive text.

+ *after a line-number* in the collations indicates that in the editions cited in the note something follows the line so numbered in the text. Thus, for example, the Quartos of *Richard III* have an additional line, not found in the Folio and not incorporated in my text, after III. vii. 219. Here my note would run

219+ *Glo.* O do not sweare my Lord of Buckingham. **Qq, Camb., Tho.**: *om.* **F1–Mal.**

If the insertion is before the beginning of a scene the reference will be given as +1. Thus *Richard III*, III. iii, opens in Qq with a line which does not appear in F1, and which I do not print. This appears in the collation as follows:

+1 *Ratl.* Come bring foorth the prisoners. **Qq, Pope±**: *om.* **F1–Rowe, Cap.**

±. As a modification of the + sign I have sometimes used ± to indicate a general agreement among the editions ordinarily collated *with certain exceptions noted*. This sign has proved to be particularly useful in *Richard III*, where the Cambridge edition differs from all others which I have collated in generally preferring the Quarto reading to that of the Folio. Thus in I. ii. 210, I follow F1 in reading 'That it may please you', this being also the reading of Rowe, Pope, Theobald, Johnson, Capell, Malone, and Thompson (the Arden editor). The Quartos, however, read 'That it would please thee', in which they are followed by the Cambridge editors. I give simply

210 may . . . you] **F1±**: would . . . thee **Qq, Camb.**

which not only presents the facts in the smallest possible space, but emphasizes the almost universal agreement of the editors in preferring the Folio text.

( ). Round brackets are used in the collation notes for several purposes and it is important that these should be understood. It may be said that their *general* significance is always to indicate a reading which is not *identical* with one which is given but which is *substantially* the same in meaning or intention so far as the purpose of the note is concerned.

It appears to me that the usual method of giving all variant readings in full, however little they differ from one another, especially when these variant readings are simply strung together in the chronological order of their appearance, is essentially inconvenient and indeed misleading, in that the method suggests a number of independent variants, whereas often the truth is that there are not actually more than two or three which embody different ideas or intentions, the remainder being no more than slight differences of presentation. A string of readings differing only by comparatively unimportant details of punctuation, &c., or some of which differ from others merely by containing misprints, is generally so repellent that few readers make any use of it.

For this reason I have endeavoured, whenever it could be done without too much complication, to *group* the readings, placing together those which are essentially or in intention similar, even though they may show minor differences. Thus in *Richard III*, III. vii. 33, we have

> But nothing spake Q1–5, Camb.
> But nothing speake Q6
> But nothing spoke F1±

It seems almost certain that 'speake' (Q6) is a misprint, and under the rule mentioned on p. 79 it would therefore have been possible to ignore it, or rather to treat it as if the reading were identical with that of Q5, and to give

> spoke] F1± : spake Qq, Camb.

As, however, here the 'misprint' is a real word, this might be regarded as incorrect. At the same time it would be both wasteful of space and actually misleading to give

> spoke] F1± : spake Q1–5, Camb.: speake Q6

as this suggests what I may call a 'genuine' variant reading in Q6. I therefore give

> 33 spoke] F1± : spake Qq (speake Q6), Camb.

indicating that there are, in my judgement, only two variants, 'spoke' and 'spake'.

Again in *Richard III*, II. ii. 3, we have two distinct readings in Qq and Ff:

> Why doe you wring your hands Qq
> Why do you weepe so oft F2–4

but F1 (the copy-text), by an evident slip, omits 'you' and has

> Why do weepe so oft

It would be cumbersome to give the readings of F1 and F2 separately and would also suggest that they are really different in intention, which they evidently are not. I therefore print 'Why do you weepe so oft' and give the note

> 3 Why . . . oft] F1± (*om.* you F1): Why doe you wring your hands Qq, Camb.

This means that F1 has in intention the reading of the lemma, though it accidentally drops 'you' and that F2 and later editors, with the exception of the Cambridge editors, have the reading of my text.

This use of brackets may be extended to deal with variants which are evidently sub-variants of others. Thus in *Richard III*, IV. v. 16, we have the following groups of readings:

> moe of noble fame Qq, Camb.
> other of great name F1–Theo. i, Tho.
> others of great name Theo. ii, Johns.
> other of great fame Cap., Mal.

It is clear that we have here two principal readings (those of Q1 and F1) and two subsidiary variants of the reading of F1. I therefore give the note on this line as

> 16 other of great name] F1–Theo. i, (others . . . Theo. ii, Johns.), (. . . fame Cap., Mal.), Tho.: moe of noble fame Qq, Camb.

It must, however, be understood that the precise form which the collations take in any particular case must be governed by convenience. Such varied interrelationships are possible between readings that too strict adherence to a formula may at times produce very awkward results.

Round brackets enclosing a siglum are also used as a warning that

G

the edition thus indicated has a reading which differs to some extent from that of the others with which it is grouped and that the variant reading of the siglum within the brackets has *not* been recorded among my collation notes. The device is of especial utility in notes concerned with the metrical arrangement of the text. When, as frequently happens, Pope rearranged the line division of the early texts with obvious advantage but, in the process, omitted, added, or transposed a word or phrase in order to make the line run more smoothly, it would obviously be erroneous to record the change as follows:

> *One line* Pope+ : *two ll.* (. . . sir,/What . . .) F1–Rowe

as this would imply that Pope's reading was identical with that of my text. At the same time it might be unnecessary for my purpose to record the precise reading of Pope and the editors who adopted his emendation. In such cases I should therefore record

> *One line* (Pope–Johns.), Cap.+ : *two ll.* (. . . sir,/What . . .) F1–Rowe

When, however, an editor makes alterations in a line which *are* recorded in an adjacent collation note, I do not consider it necessary to give this kind of warning. Thus in *Richard III*, III. vi. 10–11, I print in my text

> Here's a good World the while. Who is so grosse,
> That cannot see this palpable deuice?

Here, in the Folio, the phrase 'Who is so grosse,' is printed as part of l. 11; in l. 10 for 'Who is' the Quartos, followed by the Cambridge editors, read 'Why whoes' and in l. 11 for 'cannot see' the Quartos read 'sees not' and the Cambridge editors 'seeth not'. I therefore give the necesssary notes as

> 10–11 *Arranged as* Qq, F2+ : *two lines* (. . . while./Who . . . that . . .) F1
> 10 Who is] F1± : Why whoes Qq, Camb.
> 11 cannot see] F1± : sees not Qq, (seeth . . . Camb.)

The real point at issue, so far as the first note is concerned, is whether the phrase 'Who is so grosse,' is metrically part of l. 10 or of l. 11, and there would be no advantage in recording my line division as that of

$$(Qq), F2(+)$$

in order to draw attention to the variant readings of the Quartos and the Cambridge edition in ll. 10–11. Had I used my round brackets to indicate the existence of variant readings which I *do* record in my notes, the reader might legitimately suspect from a notation such as

$$(Qq), F2(+)$$

the existence of other variants than those recorded, whereas, in fact, in the lines above quoted from *Richard III* no variants other than those cited (and mere misprints) exist.

Round brackets have also been extensively used in collation notes concerned with punctuation and stage directions to indicate substantial agreement with the reading cited. I shall have more to say concerning their use for this purpose below.

It should further be noted that the signs $+$ and $\pm$ may also be bracketed when they are used, as described on pp. 80–2, above, to indicate the agreement of all the ordinarily collated editions (or all with certain specified exceptions) subsequent to the one cited. In such a case $(+)$ or $(\pm)$ must be taken to indicate substantial though not exact agreement. Actually this notation is seldom used in giving verbal readings, for mere differences of spelling are of course ignored, and if readings differ by more than a difference of spelling it is usually necessary to indicate the difference. The signs are, however, as will be seen later, very useful in connexion with punctuation and stage directions.

Lastly, in some plays, I have inserted within round brackets the symbol ||: e.g. (|| Q1, Pope). This is intended as a warning that, although the editions thus indicated support the reading in question, the *context* in which their reading occurs is not identical with that of the other texts which lie outside the brackets. The device saves the recording of superfluous matter among the notes to those plays of which a bad Quarto exists. Here it occasionally happens, as in *Romeo and Juliet*, that a good and bad Quarto concur in a questionable reading, or at least in a reading which has been questioned by later editors, but the support of the good Quarto reading by the bad is not so absolute as it would be if the contexts of their readings were identical. As it is not my purpose to record the numerous variants between such texts, I therefore use this symbol as a warning that unrecorded differences in the contexts of the word or words in question exist.

[ ]. Square brackets in the collation notes[1] have occasionally been used to enable the reader to envisage the more easily how additional

---

[1] This is, of course, a different matter from the use of square brackets in my *text*, which I have already explained above, p. 39.

matter links on. Thus in *Richard III*, iv. v, the Quartos insert, after l. 19, a couple of lines corresponding to iv. v. 6–8 of the Folio. As I follow the Folio arrangement in my text I record the Quarto reading in the necessary context as follows:

> 19+ [him,] Tell him, the Queene hath hartelie consented,/He shall espouse Elizabeth her daughter, **Qq, Cap.–Camb.** *Cf. ll.* 6–8

The bracketed 'him,' is from the Quartos and, besides being an additional indication of the precise place of the insertion, serves to show how it is joined to what precedes. At iv. v. 6–8, I shall, of course, have recorded the fact that the Folio lines are omitted by the Quartos, followed by Capell, Malone, and the Cambridge editors.

Square brackets are also occasionally used when this seemed the most convenient way of indicating which of two similar words or phrases is the subject of the collation. Thus in *Richard II*, i. iii. 14, is the line

> Speake truly on thy knighthoode, and thy oth.

and it is necessary to indicate that the second 'thy' appears as 'thine' in certain editions. I therefore print

> 14 [and] thy] **Qq, Cap.+**: thine **Fi–Johns.**

It is, of course, to be understood that the variants do not refer to the part of the lemma within the brackets.

– is used for 'to' and indicates the agreement of the intervening editions 'generally collated'. Thus 'Rowe–Cap.' indicates the agreement of Rowe, Pope, Theobald, Johnson, and Capell, but not necessarily of Hanmer and Warburton.

∼ in collations of *punctuation* may, if necessary, be used to obviate the necessity of repeating the preceding word. Thus in *3 Henry VI*, iii. iii. 90, where I read 'gotten?' the collation

> 90 gotten: **Fi**, (∼; **F2–Pope**)[1]

indicates that F2–Pope use a semicolon in place of the colon of Fi. Actually here my query is Theobald's, but the necessity of replacing the original colon by a question-mark being obvious, I do not regard it necessary to give a full collation.

&c. after a line number indicates 'throughout the scene'. Thus in *2 Henry VI*, i. ii,

> 17 &c. **s.n.** *Glost.*] *Hum.* **Ff**[2]

---

[1] For the absence of the lemma in this collation see p. 75.

[2] The abbreviations s.n. and s.d. in the collations are, of course, used for 'speaker's name' and 'stage direction'.

indicates that *as a speaker's name* throughout the scene (actually in
ll. 17, 25, 41, 55, and 59) the Folios have *Hum.* (or *Hu.*) in place of
Glost.

ʌ is used in giving collations of punctuation in order to indicate the
absence of punctuation of any sort. Thus such a collation as in
Richard III, ii. iii. 18,

18 wot ʌ Fɪ (full line), 2

would indicate that in the Folio the word 'wot' was not followed by a
stop of any kind, and would draw attention to the fact that the
recording of the absence of this stop was the sole purpose of the collation. In this particular case the reason for the absence of the stop is
almost certainly the fact that the line was a full one and room could
not conveniently be made for it. In this case, as frequently, F2 followed Fɪ in having no stop, though the line in that edition happens
to be less full.

COLLATION OF PUNCTUATION

Certain of the editors have had, apparently, strong and widely
differing views about punctuation. Theobald tended to many commas,
Capell to dashes and marks of exclamation; later editors generally
substitute marks of exclamation for those of interrogation in rhetorical
questions; and so on. If, therefore, when it was necessary to give
collations of punctuation in order to indicate a real change of sense
or construction, one had to give the actual punctuation of the later
editors, the collation notes would be of great length and complexity.
One of the simpler examples of this may be given. It illustrates a
frequent reason for giving punctuation-collation, namely the attach-
ing of a clause falling between two other clauses to the wrong one.
In *3 Henry VI*, v. iii. 22–4, the Folio text is as follows:

> And as we march, our strength will be augmented:
> In euery Countie as we goe along,
> Strike vp the Drumme, cry courage, and away.

It is here fairly obvious that the punctuation is incorrect and that the
line 'In euery Countie as we goe along,' should be taken with the one
which precedes it and not with the one which follows. In accordance
with this Rowe reads

> And as we march, our strength will be augmented,
> In every Country as we go along:

(his 'Country' and italic colon being doubtless misprints, as they were corrected in later editions).

Pope and Theobald read

> And as we march, our strength will be augmented
> In every county as we go along:

Johnson has

> And as we march, our strength will be augmented
> In every county as we go along.

Capell, Malone 1790, Steevens, and Dyce have

> And, as we march, our strength will be augmented
> In every county as we go along.—

Lastly, Cambridge and Hart have

> And, as we march, our strength will be augmented
> In every county as we go along.

Thus even if we neglect the variations within the line, which are indeed of no significance, we have

| augmented: | augmented, | augmented | augmented | augmented |
| along, | along: | along: | along. | along.— |

For practical purposes, however, all the last four are identical, in that they alter the relationship of the line 'In . . . along,' to its neighbours, so that instead of being linked with the preceding line it is linked with the one which follows. The note that would most simply explain the position is something to the following effect:

> 22–3 augmented: . . . along, **Ff**: **Rowe** and all later eds. punctuate so as to link line 23 to line 22 instead of to line 24.

Explanatory notes of this kind are, however, out of place among formal collations, and I therefore give the note in the following form:

> 22–3 augmented, . . . along:] **Rowe**(+): augmented: . . . along, **Ff**

The symbol +, as already noted, means editions generally collated after the one last named, and the brackets imply 'substantially' and as regards the apparent purpose of the collation.

But even this method of indicating the substantial agreement of editors is unnecessarily cumbersome in many cases. Thus in *2 Henry VI*, III. ii. 159, the Folio reads:

> What instance giues Lord Warwicke for his vow.

Here, like F2 and all later editors, I substitute an interrogation mark for the Folio stop after 'vow' and all that is really needed is a warning that I depart from the copy-text, as, indeed, any editor is bound to do in such a case. I therefore give the collation note as

159 vow. F1

There are also cases in which, while the copy-text has a punctuation which gives the sense probably intended, other texts have one which though differing slightly is not impossible—those cases, in fact, in which though the general sense is clear the exact weight to be given to the clauses is obviously a matter of opinion. An example of this kind is to be found in *1 Henry VI*, 1. iv. 73, where Talbot exhorts the dying Salisbury as follows in the Folio:

Speake *Salisbury*; at least, if thou canst, speake:

Here Pope and later editors omit the comma after 'canst', rendering the line in my opinion so commonplace that I feel bound to retain the reading of the copy-text. I record, however, the reading of Pope and later editors, since it gives what is essentially a variant reading of the line, as

73 canst ‸ Pope+

I have not, of course, recorded those changes made by modern editors which I have already referred to, in connexion with my treatment of the text, on pp. 43–4. I have regarded the moving of the question mark of an early text to the close of the sentence, the substitution of the now customary dash (to indicate an uncompleted speech) for the earlier period, and, in general, all such changes in pointing as seem to represent differences in convention and date, as attempted modernization and consequently outside the scope of my collation notes. Thus, to take a simple example, when a character enters and inquires, in reply to a summons, 'My Lord', the phrase is often terminated by a period in the early text. Certain modern editors normally point with a question mark, others with a mark of exclamation. No possible profit would be derived from encumbering my notes with observations of this character.

COLLATION OF ACT AND SCENE DIVISION

I have, of course, recorded all the divisions made in the Folio, whether these are those now recognized or not, and I have also recorded important differences in the act and scene divisions of later editions, excepting the new scenes made by Pope and the editors

who followed him in this, namely Hanmer, Warburton, and Johnson.[1]
Important differences in the division of the plays are discussed in the
introductions to the several plays, but as a general rule all that matters
to the reader is to know what authority lies behind the scene divisions
of his text and how far these divisions correspond with those of the
principal editions. Collations are therefore generally given in the form

I. iii.] *New scene* **Pope+** : *not divided* **F1–Rowe**

The fact that the scene may be differently numbered in different
editions is ignored, unless, of course, the numbering of my text
does not tally with that of the copy-text, in which case the reading of
the copy-text would be given: as, for example, in *Richard III,*

IV. iv.] *New scene* **F1±** (*Scena Tertia.* **F1**): *not divided* **Qq, Theo.**

The truth is that no method of comparing the scene distribution
of different editions is satisfactory save a tabular one, and in view of
the number of scene divisions made by Pope such tables have to be
lengthy and elaborate, while their utility is not really very great. On
the comparatively few occasions when one requires to refer to a
passage in an early text, a knowledge of the act and scene is seldom
of much assistance, as in any case the lines are not numbered in any
edition[2]—so far as I know—earlier than that of the Cambridge editors,
1863–6.

In the introduction to each play I have called attention to such
facts concerning the scene divisions of the various editions as seem
to have any bearing on the editors' interpretation of the action.

COLLATION OF STAGE DIRECTIONS

The stage directions of the various editions, especially those of
the eighteenth century, present some difficulty in that they are so
constantly varied in wording without much, if any, difference being
made in the meaning. My rule has been to ignore *mere* differences in

---

[1] The scene divisions are generally identical in these editions, but there are a few
minor variations. They were based on the Continental method of marking a new
scene whenever an important character enters or leaves the stage, with the result
that they are much more numerous than those of later editors, whose divisions are
based on either the occurrence of a change of locality or the stage being left empty.

[2] At any rate, any edition of the complete works. Some single plays may have
been issued earlier with numbered lines, but I know of none. The custom of
indenting speeches which formed the second part of lines of verse, without which the
numbering of verse lines on the modern principle would have been troublesome,
seems to have begun with Steevens's edition of 1793.

wording[1] but to record anything which seems to imply a real difference in the editor's conception of the conduct of the play. For example, consider the stage direction at *Richard III*, I. ii. 226.

The stage has been occupied by a coffin containing the corpse of King Henry VI with a guard of halberdiers and presumably also a party of bearers, the Lady Anne, and Richard, Duke of Gloucester. At the point in question Lady Anne has just retired from the scene, together with two gentlemen, Tressel and Barkley, leaving the corpse with an indefinite number of attendants, and Richard. Richard now, at least in the Quartos, says 'Sirs take vp the corse' and orders the bearers to convey it to Whitefriars, he himself remaining to soliloquize.

The directions of the Quartos, Folios, and certain later editors are as follows:

> *Exeunt. manet Gl.* Qq.
> *Exit Coarse* Ff, Rowe, Pope.
> *Exeunt with the Coarse.* Theobald, Johnson.
> *Exeunt the rest, with the Corpse.* Capell.
> *Exeunt the rest, with the corse.* Malone.
> *Exeunt all but Gloucester.* Cambridge, Thompson.

In a case like this, I think that there is no real need to depart from the copy-text, which is here F1. No reader is likely to interpret '*Exit Coarse*' to mean that the corpse walked out alone, or even that it was merely removed by one or two persons. The meaning is quite obviously that the funeral procession as a whole moved on. It seems, therefore, legitimate to suppose that there is no real difference of opinion among editors as to the movements of the different characters, and in this particular case nothing would be gained by presenting the reader with the various directions of Theobald and later editors.

In accordance with my object, which is, as explained above, to record only such variations from the copy-text as seem to imply a real difference in an editor's conception of the conduct of the play, I have therefore disregarded the following:

(*a*) Mere differences in wording such as the substitution of an indicative for an imperative. Thus if the copy-text reads '*Kisse her*', the now customary substitution of '*He kisses her*' is not recorded.

---

[1] Further, I ignore differences of typographical form in citing stage directions in the collations, giving them all in italics. In the original texts there is much variation and perhaps even more in the conventions followed by later editors. See p. 51.

(*b*) Explanatory additions. Thus if the copy-text read '*Prince*' and there was no reasonable doubt as to the identity of the prince intended, I should regard it as unnecessary to include a note to the effect that Rowe, followed by later editors, substituted '*Prince of Wales*'. Similarly, should it have proved necessary to add some such explanatory addition to the stage directions of my text in order to bring the name by which a character was referred to in his entry into line with his speech prefixes in the scene (see p. 55), I should likewise not record the editor who first made such addition. Thus in *1 Henry VI*, I. vi, where I print '[*Charles the*] *Dolphin*', in order to facilitate recognition that the Folio's '*Dolphin*' is the character who speaks as '*Char.*', no collation note is given.[1]

(*c*) Nor do I record among the collation notes variations in nomenclature for the same character found among later editions. Thus, if my copy-text described a character as 'Richard' and later editors had preferred his title 'Gloucester', I should regard the difference as irrelevant to the purposes of my notes.

(*d*) Nor do I record the alterations of later editors in the order in which characters are enumerated unless the changes they make appear to show a pointedly different conception of the manner of an entry. Thus if the copy-text had an entry for nobles and prelates in haphazard order and later editors had enumerated these in accordance with their rank and calling, no notice would be taken of such alteration unless it seemed to embody a deliberate attempt to suggest a significant division into parties, &c., with some bearing on the play's plot and the action of the scene.

In the following cases a partial collation is all that has seemed to me necessary:

(*a*) Where the copy-text has been emended, but the necessity for alteration is apparent. Thus where the copy-text has '*Exit.*' and '*Exeunt.*' is patently required and substituted in my text, I record

S.D. Exit. Ff

(*b*) Where a significant addition has been made to the stage directions of the copy-text all that I record are the first and subsequent

---

[1] In *1 Henry VI*, III. iv, however, where in the head entry the Folio omits to mention Vernon and Basset, and I add these characters to the stage direction, I necessarily record that this addition was made by Capell and subsequent editors.

editors to make such addition. Thus:

s.d. *He dies.*] Hanm., Cap.+

The fact that additions to the copy-text stage directions are placed within square brackets in my text will already have informed the reader that the stage direction is an editorial addition.

(*c*) Where, in the interests of uniformity, it has proved necessary to replace the copy-text name by another (substantially its equivalent) I give the collation note as follows:

s.d. *Armado*] *Braggart* Ff

The primary object of such notes is, of course, to record the fact that the copy-text reading has been altered and the section on Dramatis Personae in the introduction to the particular play will contain all relevant information concerning the nomenclature preferred by Rowe and later editors. I therefore carry the variant readings no farther than F4.

By thus eliminating from my collation notes on stage directions insignificant variations and explanatory additions, and by recording, with the minimum of superfluous information, the necessary facts concerning the correction of patent errors and the additions I have considered it advisable to make in my text, I hope I have made it easier for the reader to concentrate on essential differences in editorial opinion concerning the conduct of the play. Such are, principally, the addition of the names of characters whose presence is indicated by the dialogue of a scene, though not by its directions (e.g. Capell's addition of Vernon and Basset mentioned above[1]), differences of opinion concerning the characters who leave the stage at a particular point in the action, and such additions as embody significant inferences concerning the manner of an entry or an exit. Examples will be found below.

In view of the constant slight changes made by the editors,[2] I have found it necessary in the collation of stage directions to make much use of the round brackets referred to above, in order to indicate *substantial* though not verbal agreement of later editions with those cited. I have been able by this means to effect a very great economy in the complexity of the notes without, I hope, detracting in the smallest degree from their value.

---

[1] See p. 92, n. 1.
[2] Capell in particular had a great fondness for rewriting the directions.

Thus, to give a simple example, in *3 Henry VI*, IV. viii. 32, where the Folio has merely '*Exeunt*' and it would not be immediately apparent to a reader that all except King Henry and Exeter had left the stage, I give the direction, following the Cambridge editors, as '*Exeunt [all but King Henry and Exeter]*'. Capell, followed by Malone, has a direction to the same effect which enumerates, however, not the characters who remain on the stage but those who leave. I therefore give the note

32 S.D. *all but . . . Exeter*] (**Cap.**, **Mal.**), **Camb.**, **Hart**

Had I cited the precise wording of Capell's direction it would have given the reader the unnecessary trouble of determining for himself that the directions of Capell and the Cambridge editors were substantially identical without adding anything of importance to my note.

As a somewhat more complicated example I may cite the directions found in the various editions at *2 Henry VI*, I. iii. 171.

Enter Armorer and his Man. Ff.
Enter Horner *the Armorer, and his Man* Peter. Rowe, Pope.
Enter Horner *the Armorer, and his Man* Peter, *guarded.* Theobald, Johnson, Cambridge, Hart.
Enter Servants of Suffolk, *bringing in the* Armorer, *and his* Man. Capell.
Enter Servants of Suffolk, *bringing in* Horner *and* Peter. Malone.

Following my general rule of adding the names of characters who have personal names elsewhere in the play, and of omitting attendants, &c., when the presence of these is obvious, I give the direction in the form:

Enter [Horner the] Armorer and his Man [Peter].

It is not in accordance with my principles to record the fact that I follow Rowe and certain later editors in adding the purely explanatory addition that the Armourer is Horner and that his Man is Peter; nor does it matter in the least—so far as the conduct of the play is concerned—that Capell failed to make this addition. The essential differences between the reading of my text and those of later editors are (*a*) that Theobald, followed substantially by all later editors, described Peter as entering '*guarded*', and (*b*) that Capell and Malone envisaged the guard as consisting of Suffolk's men. I therefore give the note

171 S.D. *. . . Peter, guarded.* **Theo.**(+): *Enter Servants of Suffolk, bringing in the Armorer, and his Man.* **Cap.**, (**Mal.**)

I should perhaps add, concerning my use of brackets, that I have considered it unnecessary to indicate by this means differences in the various editions which consist of no more than the abbreviation, or the expansion of the abbreviation, of a name or the substitution of an alternative name for the same character. Thus *'Exeunt Mercutio and Benvolio'* would be regarded as equivalent to *'Ex. Mer., Ben.'*, and in a play where Gloucester and Humphrey were merely alternative names for the same character I should regard *'Ex. Hum.'*, *'Exit Glou.'*, and *'Exit Gloster'* as identical.

Further, no notice has been taken in the collations of the varied practice of editors in giving or omitting the *name* of a person who leaves the stage at the end of his speech. As explained on p. 51, in all cases where the person referred to by *'Exit'* is clear, I follow the general practice of the early texts and do not add the name. Suppose, then, that (in agreement with later editors) I regard as necessary an exit first given by Theobald in the form *'Exit Smith.'*: my note would have the form

Exit.] Theo.+

Lastly, Capell and, in a far greater degree, Dover Wilson have attempted to add picturesqueness to the plays by elaborating the stage directions. Dover Wilson in particular often substitutes such phrases as 'Rosaline runs away', 'She flings out', 'They march off' for the simple *'Exit'* or *'Exeunt'*. I have treated all such fanciful variations as equivalent to the conventional forms.

COLLATION OF SPEAKERS' NAMES

In common with Rowe and all subsequent editors, I have attempted uniformity in the giving of the speakers' names, which in some of the early editions are extremely irregular (see p. 57). I have accordingly chosen *one* form of the name of each character—generally the one by which he is addressed or referred to at his first entrance—and have used this in the speech-headings throughout.[1] I have, however, recorded in the collation notes the *names* given in the copy-text whenever I have substituted another (sometimes in the form of a note referring to the whole scene), but not the variations in the form of the name. Thus in *2 Henry VI*, I have called Humphrey, Duke of Gloucester, as a speaker *'Glost.'* throughout, but when in any scene

---

[1] Save, of course, where a character changes his name in the course of a play owing to his elevation to higher rank.

the form in the Folio is '*Humf.*' I have recorded this, though I have *not* noted the variations in the abbreviations, such as '*Hum.*' or '*Hu.*'. These are regarded as non-significant variations and are in all cases ignored, as are all misprints except when these consist in the substitution of one speaker's name for another.

Though I regard the substitution of one name for another as a matter which must be recorded in the collation notes, I have not thought it necessary to record among the collations the explanatory additions (such as the provision of a titulary prefix) which it has sometimes been necessary to make in order to secure uniformity in the speakers' names of my text. Thus if the copy-text read *Iohn* in a text where I had adopted *K. Iohn* as speech-prefix, I should add the necessary prefix *K.* without drawing attention to the fact that this was my addition either in the text or in the collation notes. If, on the other hand, I had adopted the prefix *Iohn* and my copy-text read *K. Iohn* I should likewise silently drop the titulary prefix. The substitution of *Iohn* for *King* or vice versa would, however, be collated in the manner already described. Should there be any ambiguity in a play as to which John was meant, it would of course be necessary to give collation notes on explanatory additions I had made.

Variations in the names given to the speakers in editions other than the copy-text are also generally ignored in the collations, provided that there is no doubt that the person intended is the same. The various names given to the characters by modern editors will be found recorded in the introductions to the several plays under 'Dramatis Personae'.

COLLATION OF LOCALITIES

After much hesitation and a number of experiments I have come to the conclusion that anything like a full verbal collation of the localities as given in the various editions which I have generally collated for the text would occupy space quite disproportionate to its value. There is as a rule agreement in all essentials, but at the same time innumerable differences in details of wording. What one calls a wood, another will call a forest, a third a park, and so on, when no more is meant than a place where there are or may be animals which can be hunted. Some editors seem to feel a far greater need for precision than others. In particular Capell for a simple indication such as 'The Palace' will as a rule substitute some such phrase as 'A Room of State in the Palace'—though it might surely be taken for granted that if great personages meet in a palace to discuss affairs of state, their meeting will take place in an appropriate room and not, for example, in the kitchen! Such particularization seems otiose, as would, I think, be the attempt to record it in detail.

In certain modern editions such as Professor Dover Wilson's a further step in localization is attempted. Professor Wilson envisages the modern theatre with all its scenic resources, and supposes climbable trees, lanes, lofty turrets,[1] and the like. Such 'scenery' is perhaps not out of place in a modernized text for a modern reader, inasmuch as it may represent what was in Shakespeare's mind as he wrote and what he would have wished for in the way of setting if this had been practicable in his day. It is, however, quite impossible to record elaborations such as these without rendering the collations exceedingly long and complicated, and I have therefore as a rule been compelled to ignore all such localizations except when they seem to involve a new interpretation of the action.

When, therefore, there appears to be substantial agreement as to the locality of any scene I have, as explained at p. 60, above, generally noted this as it appears in the Cambridge edition. At the same time I have, in the introduction to the plays, given some account of the general contributions made to the locality headings by the various editors. In the few cases in which there is any real difference of opinion as to where a scene is laid I have of course recorded the various views, generally, as the difference can seldom be made clear by formal collations, in an explanatory note.

COLLATION OF LINE ARRANGEMENT

Something has already been said concerning my treatment of errors and abnormalities in the line division of the early texts.[2] A further difficulty, which affects more particularly the collation notes, must be mentioned here. We find verse turnovers arranged in the Folio in the three following ways:

(a) *Som.* Yorke set him on, Yorke should haue sent him
ayde. (*1 Hen. VI*, IV. iv. 29)

---

[1] e.g. 'A wall, with a postern, behind the Duke's palace: inside a strip of garden dividing the wall from a lofty turret; outside, a narrow lane with bushes: a moonlit night' (*Two Gentlemen*, IV. ii.).

[2] See pp. 44–9, above.

    (*b*) *Qu.* Come, come, we know your meaning Brother
                            (Gloster
                         (*Rich. III*, I. iii. 73)
                            (ther
    Queen. Theres a good mother boy, that blots thy fa-
                         (*K. John*, II. i. 132)
    (*c*) *Spirit.* Aske what thou wilt; that I had sayd, and
    done.   (*2 Hen. VI*, I. iv. 27)

The first two arrangements seem to be normally used for verse alone, whereas the last is indifferently used both for prose and verse. The Cambridge editors in their collation notes described some of the lines arranged in the form of example (*c*) as intended for prose in the Folio (as, for example, *2 Henry VI*, I. iv. 27, 28, II. i. 15, 81[1]), though at other times (as in *2 Henry VI*, I. iii. 175, II. i. 62, 101, 108, 110[2]) they ignore the Folio arrangement. I can see no consistency in their practice and when I have no doubt that verse was intended, as when such turnovers occur in a verse context and the line belongs to a verse-speaking character, I have ignored the typographical ambiguity. Where doubt as to what was intended exists I have, of course, recorded the Folio arrangement. That the Folio cannot seriously have intended many of these apparently ambiguous turnovers as prose is evident from their occurrence in texts set up from Quartos where no doubt whatsoever could have existed in the compositor's mind as to the verse character of the line (see, for example, *The Merchant of Venice*, III. ii. 240, 241, where the Folio turns over unmistakably verse lines of Q1 in this manner).

THE INTRODUCTIONS

    In the introductions to the several plays I have, after giving brief descriptions of the early Quarto editions,[3] discussed at such length as seemed to be necessary the relationship between the early editions, with a view to determining which text should be used as the basis of mine, and what probability there is that any of the derivative texts contains readings of Shakespearian authority.

---

[1] I. iv. 28, 29, II. i. 15, 81 in the Cambridge edition.
[2] I. iii. 178, II. i. 62, 101, 109, 111 in the Cambridge edition.
[3] The work of Professor A. W. Pollard in his *Shakespeare Folios and Quartos*, 1909, and the forthcoming very full bibliography of the English Drama to 1640 by Dr. W. W. Greg render it superfluous for an editor to give bibliographical details of Shakespearian plays in future editions, but it may be useful to give for reference full titles or the main facts concerning the different editions.

I have also discussed the date of writing of the several plays and of any revision which is thought to have taken place, and have briefly summarized the various opinions, or what seem the most important of these, as to the authorship of those plays which have been regarded as not, or only in part, the work of Shakespeare. I have, however, not attempted to go into these latter questions in any detail nor have I discussed the arguments for or against the various views, as this seems to me no necessary part of the duty of an editor of the texts as we have them, as well as being singularly futile in view of the lack of evidence.[1] Further, although I have summarized recent opinions on the history of Shakespeare's manuscripts before they got into print, in view of the interest of the subject and the prominence which has lately been given to it, I have made no attempt at full discussion. As stated above (p. 9), I myself doubt if, in the absence of external evidence, sufficient certainty can be reached on the subject of the manuscripts to make such researches more than interesting speculations.

The sources of the plays have been briefly dealt with, but I have made no attempt to discuss Shakespeare's use of them in any detail. So far as possible I have avoided speculative matter such as questions of possible topical allusions and of whether characters were intended to represent, either for purposes of flattery or satire, eminent persons of their time, though I have, so far as could be done in brief, mentioned such views of scholars as I have found presented in a reasoned manner.

In other sections of each introduction I have discussed the division into acts and scenes, the localities assigned to the scenes by various editors, and the names given by them to the various characters. In the case of the historical plays I have added a kind of *Who's Who*. I must confess, for my own part, that I found the respective relationships of the numerous exalted personages exceedingly difficult to disentangle and to remember, and it seemed to me that much trouble might be saved to readers by brief accounts of them so far as they enter into the plays. I have naturally commented upon the more

---

[1] It seems to me that we are far from possessing a sufficient number of plays which can be indubitably assigned to Shakespeare's contemporaries as their unmixed work for it to be possible to judge whether work attributed to them must, or even might, be theirs. Further, the proportion of extant to non-extant plays, at any rate before 1600, is probably quite small, and even of the authors whose names we know there are several about the characteristics of whose work we are completely ignorant.

important departures from orthodox chronology or history which the plays contain. Instead, however of giving, as is often done, a summary of the history of the period of each play in the introduction, in order that readers may see how Shakespeare handles and modifies it—a matter which may easily be studied, for the English plays, in Boswell-Stone's well-known *Shakespeare's Holinshed*—I have added at the head of each scene a brief note on the historical events dealt with. It seemed to me that this would be much more helpful to the reader than if he had to refer back from the scene which he was reading to a general summary.

I have made no attempt whatever to deal with the representation of the plays or with their stage history unless this bears on other problems, such as the localities or act and scene divisions: nor have I attempted anything of the nature of aesthetic criticism.

THE EXPLANATORY NOTES

The notes in this edition are principally of three kinds.

1. *Textual.* These are intended to discuss difficult or doubtful readings, and so far as possible to justify the readings adopted in the text. In many cases they are of course also to some extent explanatory, as in discussing a reading it is frequently necessary to explain the meaning which is or may be attached to it.

2. *Glossarial or explanatory.* I have also attempted to deal with difficulties of meaning. I have not, however, thought it necessary to gloss ordinary Elizabethan words used with their normal significations. It seemed to me that, in an edition of this sort which is unlikely to be used by those who have not at least a knowledge of the language of the Authorized Version of the Bible and some reading in Elizabethan literature, to attempt to gloss every word used in a sense in which it is not now used would be not only otiose but irritating to the reader Such words as *still* (= always), *presently* (immediately), *prevent* (= anticipate), *swain* (= yokel), *sort* (= group, number), and so on, occur of course hundreds of times and to gloss them every time would be very wasteful of space. I have therefore assumed that the reader will either be familiar with them or will have some dictionary or Shakespearian glossary to which he can turn in any difficulty. I am, however, giving a brief glossarial list of such words as are not explained in their contexts at the end of each volume, with the minimum of explanation.

At the same time, in a number of cases when the meaning of a particular word in the context seemed doubtful or when the phrases seemed particularly liable to be misunderstood by a modern reader, I have added such brief comment as seemed advisable.

Further, in certain cases where the original has a spelling which might not easily be identified by the reader with the modern form of the word intended, or where one of two or more different words might be substituted in modern texts, I have given a note such as

trauail, i.e. travel (Pope+)

meaning that Pope and later editions print 'travel' (and not 'travail', which might equally well be signified by the Elizabethan spelling). For the reason set out on p. 64, I do not regard such notes as in their place among the collations, in that there is no question of error in the original readings; the forms given by the later editions being not of the nature of correction, but of simple modernization, which it seems to me important to keep distinct from real differences of reading.

3. I have also dealt in these notes with certain difficulties as regards the action of the plays, the supposed localities, the division into acts and scenes, and such other matters, but only so far as these affect the text and its interpretation. Illustrative quotations, parallels from other plays, and the like are excluded from the plan of this edition.

APPENDIX A

MINOR TYPOGRAPHICAL ABNORMALITIES, ETC.

THE following rules have been adopted in dealing with certain minor typographical abnormalities of the early editions.

Doubtful (damaged) letters. Certain letters when damaged resemble others. Thus an e of which the cross-bar is broken resembles a c; an f badly worn may resemble ſ; an l broken in the middle may resemble i, and so on. In such cases when there can be no doubt what is meant I have generally given the printer the benefit of the doubt. It seems absurd to print such a note as

heauen] perhaps hcauen Fɪ

Of course, if doubt as to what was intended is possible, the difficulty is noted.

Turned letters. (*a*) Certain letters when turned resemble other letters unturned. Thus

turned n resembles u

,, u ,, n

,, d ,, p

,, p ,, d

,, b ,, q

,, q ,, b

Further, a turned and worn a resembles e, and vice versa.

In the case of these letters, when the letter which at first sight appears to be the one printed is obviously what was intended, that letter is printed and the error is not recorded in the collations; thus

prince is printed as prince

house ,, ,, house

quote ,, ,, quote

without comment, as it is quite evident what is meant. If, however, we had a word like 'out', the second letter being a turned n, where the sense required 'ont' or where 'ont' was a possible reading as an alternative to 'out', I should, whether I read 'out' or 'ont' in the text, give a note indicating that the copy-text had 'out (*turned* n)'.

It is, as a matter of fact, in many cases, impossible to be sure in Elizabethan printing, especially if the type is much worn, whether the letter actually is n or turned u, p or turned d, and so on, and it would, where there is no possible doubt of the reading intended, be otiose to encumber one's notes with quantities of collations which add nothing to the reader's information and which in many cases would have to be marked with a query.

(*b*) In the case of the majority of letters, which when the type is turned do not resemble any other letter, the turning is simply ignored. Thus 'ɔome' would be printed as 'come' without any comment.

Wrong-fount letters. Wrong-fount letters which are evidently merely accidental, such as a black-letter or italic type in a roman word, or a roman type in an italic word, are corrected and the errors ignored, as is also erroneous black-letter or italic punctuation.

In a similar way italic *A*, *a*, *I*, *O*, and *o* standing as single words in a roman context are silently corrected, as would be the same words appearing in roman type in an italic context.

Whole words, other than the above-mentioned, printed in italic type when roman was to be expected, are either printed as they stand or corrected according to circumstances. In the latter case the original form is given in a collation note.

Occasional letters of a wrong size are corrected and the error ignored.

Omission of capitals. We sometimes find lines which are evidently meant as verse printed in verse lines but without a capital at the beginning of the lines. These are here provided with capitals in the text and if they only occur occasionally each change made is indicated in a collation note. There are, however, certain plays such as *The Merchant of Venice* in the copy-text of which a large part of the verse is without capitals. In such a case the lines are given capitals in accordance with normal practice, and a general note is added at the first place where the change is made calling attention to their frequent absence in the original.

Songs, &c., occurring in the plays. Songs, poems, and other incidental verse intended to be sung or read aloud are in the early texts printed in a variety of ways, even in a single scene, sometimes in the ordinary type of the text, sometimes in italics, and sometimes in a smaller size of type. There seemed no object in following the copy-texts in such merely typographical irregularities. I have therefore given all such items in italic type, centring them if this seemed desirable, recording the type of the copytext if this has been altered. In incidental prose pieces, such as letters, and in inset plays, such as the Pyramus and Thisbe play of the *Midsummer Night's Dream*, I have not thought it necessary to depart from the type of my copy-text.

Abbreviations. I have allowed such customary abbreviations as L. (Lord), M. (Master), S. (Saint) to stand in my text and have not, of course, considered it necessary to draw attention to their expansion by later editors unless the expansion involves some difficulty of interpretation or punctuation. Personal names abbreviated in the dialogue of the copy-text (e.g. 'Rich.' for Richard) have, however, been expanded. Such lines as

The lord Northumberland, his son yong H. Percie

and

H. Bull. on both his knees doth kisse king Richards hand

seemed to me too irritating to a reader to be allowed to stand. The copy-text readings are of course in each case given in the collation notes.

On the other hand, I have not ordinarily expanded such abbreviations in the copy-text stage directions.

Place of stage directions. In the copy-texts the place of the stage directions, especially '*Exit*' and '*Exeunt*', is varied by the printer according to his convenience. Thus while the normal place for an '*Exit*' may be at the end of the final line of the character's last speech, if this line happens to be full or if for any reason he wishes to make an extra line he might place it in a line by itself, either centred or at the end. This evidently has no significance and, as it is in any case impossible always to place the directions exactly as they are in the copy-text on account of the occasional necessity of expanding them, I ignore such typographical variations as I have mentioned and place the directions where they seem most convenient and least unsightly; i.e. generally, if short, at the end of the line where they belong, or if they are too long for this in the centre of the next line. No indication of such purely typographical departures from the original is given, though of course whenever a *significant* change is made in the position of a stage direction the fact is noted.

APPENDIX B

THE DESCENT OF EDITIONS

THEORETICALLY the genetic descent of editions, i.e. their relationship to one another as printer's 'copy', is not necessarily the same as the relationship of the texts which they exhibit. Consider, for example, two editions of a certain book, A and B, the latter having been printed from the former and containing a normal number of mistakes and conjectural emendations; and suppose that the owner of a copy of B were to compare it with a copy of A and correct in it all or most of its false readings by the help of the earlier edition; and that a third edition were printed from that copy. The genetic order of the editions is evidently $A > B > C$, but so far as the *text* is concerned it is evident that C might be derived as much from A as from B. I know of no such case as this and it is hardly likely that any exists, but it seems quite possible that the occasional readings which we find reverting to a text earlier than that from which an edition appears to have been printed may be due to the copy used having been to some extent corrected from an earlier edition.[1] On the other hand, such apparent reversions may often be explained more simply as guesses of the compositor.

Ultimately, of course, what we are concerned with is *texts* of Shakespeare, not *editions*, but nevertheless when we are investigating a group of texts the foundation of our inquiry must necessarily be the genetic sequence of the editions, i.e. which of these served as 'copy' (whether corrected or not) for which other. The most frequent practice at all periods of printing was indeed that each edition except the first was printed from the one which immediately preceded it. The rule was, however, not an invariable one. Sometimes two editions were both printed from the same earlier one, and occasionally we find editions printed partly from one edition and partly from another. This might happen when a book was reprinted page for page and two compositors were working on the job at the same time. The master printer might have copies of the two preceding editions and it might be convenient to give one to each of the compositors to work from.

[1] An occasional cause of a misprint occurring in a certain edition being repeated in the next edition but one, but not in the intervening one, may be that the second of these editions was corrected at press, the misprint of the first being thus eliminated in some copies but not in others. If the third was printed from a copy of the second not containing the correction, its reading might naturally correspond with that of the first. Another possible way in which readings may seem to skip one or more editions is when a press reader uses, in correcting, an edition earlier than the one used in setting up the book. I mention these points as examples of the difficulties which sometimes may occur in connexion with what seems a very simple inquiry.

It is evident that, as a rule, little care was taken over such points. We cannot therefore take it for granted that the descent of the editions corresponds with their dates of publication and must investigate the interrelationship within the various groups for ourselves. It will, I think, save space in the introductions of the several plays to deal with the matter briefly here.

The way in which editions of a printed book are related to one another can generally be deduced with little difficulty by an examination of the books themselves. The arguments used are sometimes described as either 'literary', when the relationship is deduced by a comparison of the readings, or 'bibliographical', when the evidence is of a typographical nature. As a rule both classes of evidence are used in conjunction. A full discussion of the evidence usually to be found is unnecessary here, but a few notes and warnings may not be out of place.

The earlier editors, so far as they concerned themselves with the relationship of editions at all, seem generally to have relied solely on the evidence of readings. This, of course, is in general a perfectly satisfactory method though a very laborious one. If one has a full collation of, say, five editions of a play, inspection of this will reveal, as a rule, without much doubt which edition served as 'copy' for which other. An important point to notice is, however, that in order that fairly certain results shall be reached, it is necessary that there shall be a considerable number of variants, or at least that of whatever variants there are a considerable proportion shall be *unimportant* variants; for it is a general rule that the less significant the readings varied are, from a literary point of view, the greater is their weight as evidence of the genetic relationships of the texts in which they occur. The reason of this is, of course, that significant readings are likely to be noticed and if they look wrong to be 'corrected' by the proof-reader, with the result that such corrections may completely mask what was originally set by the compositor and thus destroy any evidence of the text from which he worked: on the other hand, mere casual and meaningless variation in punctuation, typographical arrangement, &c., is far more likely to persist untouched. It follows from this that any attempt to deduce the relationship of editions by considering the *number*[1] of variants between them can seldom be of any use unless we consider the nature of the individual variants.

The most reliable evidence as to the relationship of editions, and the easiest to use, is generally bibliographical. To begin with there is the evidence of general arrangement. If two editions correspond page for page throughout, or even in any large part, it may safely be presumed that one

[1] It is not really possible to discuss the variants between two texts numerically, on account of the many cases in which one variation entails others, e.g. when a singular subject is replaced by a plural and a string of verbal and pronominal forms have to be altered in consequence. Is this one variant or several?

descended from the other or that both descended from a common ancestor. We cannot, of course, say 'were printed' in place of 'descended', for there may have been intermediate editions. Naturally, there are other peculiarities of arrangement which may afford evidence of relationship in a similar way. The best of all evidence of the genetic connexion between editions is undoubtedly the persistence of misprints or of 'unnatural' typographical arrangement. If, for example, in two or more editions of a work 'though' is misprinted 'thought', or if in these editions a stage direction is found awkwardly placed when there would have been room for it in a more normal position, or if it is divided into two or more lines unnecessarily or is in any other way typographically unusual, it is highly probable that one or more of these texts was used as 'copy' for one or more of the others, that, in fact, we can arrange them into a genetic group; and if we find a number of similar agreements between the texts we may take the relationship as almost certain.

If we know the date of printing of the various editions we can therefore very often readily determine their genetic relationship by a consideration of the overlapping of errors. Thus if we have three editions of a book, A, B, C, and know that of these A was the first to be printed; and if we find an appreciable number of errors, or even marked peculiarities common to A and B and others common to B and C, but none common to A and C except such as are also found in B, we can infer that the genetic order must have been $A > B > C$.

If, however, B were known to have been the earliest printed, then a similar disposition of misprints would have shown that the genetic relationship must have been

$$\begin{matrix} & B & \\ & \bigwedge & \\ A & & C \end{matrix}$$

while if C were the earliest, the relationship must have been $C > B > A$.

It is important to notice that such an arrangement of misprints as this would not *by itself*, and unless it were known at least which of the editions was earliest, give us any information as to the relationship of the editions. This, however, may sometimes be determined by other considerations. For example, the three texts may all show an abnormality of some kind in the textual arrangement such as a misplaced stage direction. It may be evident on inspection that in A there is a good reason for the abnormality, but that in B and C the compositor has blindly followed an abnormal arrangement which he had before him in his 'copy' but which in *his* edition, owing perhaps to the use of a longer type-line or a slightly narrower fount of type, was no longer necessary. This would of course show that edition A was the earliest and we could deduce the relationship $A > B > C$ even if all the editions were undated.[1]

[1] Naturally of course in any investigation of this kind we should not rely on a

On the other hand, we must be careful not to assume that when two editions both correct a misprint occurring in an earlier edition one is necessarily printed from the other, for misprints are liable to be corrected quite independently by different compositors or proof-readers.

Thus suppose that in three editions, A, B, C, of which A is known to be the earliest, we find such readings as the following:

A	B	C	
eare	care	eare	('care' being evidently correct)
at one	atone	at one	('atone' being evidently correct)

we can infer that the text cannot have passed through B and that therefore the relationship of the editions must have been $A > C > B$ or $A\!\!<^{B}_{C}$, for the chance of two similar misprints occurring independently in two different editions neither of which was printed from the other is negligible.

Consider, however, a different disposition of the same readings, such as

A	B	C	
care	eare	care	('care' being evidently correct)
atone	at one	atone	('atone' being evidently correct)

This would *not* show us that C had been printed from A rather than from B, for in both cases the C reading might easily have been produced by the correction of that of B by a proof-reader. All agreements with an earlier text in a *correct* reading must indeed be treated as possible corrections of a compositor or proof-reader and their value as evidence of the interrelationship of editions in which they occur must be severely discounted.

From these simple examples it will, I think, be clear that an investigation of the genetic relationships of editions is not merely a simple matter of counting up the number of readings common to a number of editions or the number of differences between them, but as a general rule must involve a consideration of the nature of the individual readings themselves, as well as sometimes an attempt to explain how they came to occur. Cases may indeed sometimes be found of the reading of one edition being misprinted in a second and the misprint being so corrected in a third that the relation of the three, at least so far as the particular forme[1] is concerned, is clearly demonstrated by this one set of readings alone, as for example if we found

single instance as a proof of relationship, but should try to get a number of proofs all pointing in the same direction. We must always remember that different editions of a book may have served as copy for different parts of a reprint.

[1] For further information on these and similar matters, I must venture to refer readers to my *Introduction to Bibliography for Literary Students*, Oxford, 1927. The important point in all questions affecting readings of printed texts, as I believe I was the first to point out in my edition of B. Barnes's *Devil's Charter* in 1904, pp. xv–xvi, is that the unit is not the book as a whole, nor even the sheet, but the forme, i.e. the group of pages which in printing fall on one side of the sheet.

the readings 'obscured' A, 'obseured' B, 'obserued' C, where the last is evidently an unlucky attempt to correct the obvious misprint in the second.

But if the group of editions which we are investigating happens to be well printed, we cannot always find a sufficient number of misprints or typographical peculiarities to afford evidence of the relationship of the texts. In such cases we sometimes find an attempt to show the relationship by a consideration of the spellings of the various editions. Now there is little doubt that if we took *all* the words capable of variant spelling in any group of editions, or a large proportion of such words, and compared the spellings found, we could in most cases make a reasonable guess as to which edition had been printed from which, for, other things being equal, most compositors would probably follow the spelling of the copy-text more often than they departed from it. Even so, however, there are many considerations which might prevent spelling from being a safe guide. One edition might be printed in a house which had a custom of using particular spellings[1] or the compositor might have strong preferences of his own: or sometimes, perhaps, a change of type-measure might lead to the use of shorter or longer spellings in variable words. Nevertheless, if *all* the words capable of variation in a series of texts were individually examined and if in three editions, A, B, C, we found, for example, a large number of similar spellings in A and B where C varied, and a large number in B and C where A varied, and if we knew that the order of printing was A, B, C, it would be natural to suppose a genetic descent A > B > C, for if B and C had each been printed from A, then B and C would have had to make independently a large number of similar changes, which is improbable.

Any argument founded on spelling-variation becomes, however, at once very dangerous if we do not consider *all* the variations that occur between the texts but only a selection of them, those perhaps which happen to strike us as remarkable. We may have, for example, in certain texts such variations as

> portcullis—percullis; sometime—sometimes (in the sense of 'formerly');
> through—thorough; then—than (conjunction of comparison); travel—
> travail (= mod. travel); wright—write (= mod. write),

or even such strange-looking forms as 'eughe' or 'iewe' for 'yew', or 'mushrump' for 'mushroom'. Now, about 1580–90 all these would have been regarded as ordinary non-significant variants. Neither was wrong, and

---

[1] The question as to whether at this period any printing-houses had rules of their own as to spelling and other points of typographical practice has not, I think, been investigated. A hasty attempt that I made several years ago to find any cause for the unusual, and unusually consistent, spellings in R. Greene's *Euphues his Censure to Philautus*, 1587, gave a purely negative result, i.e. I could find no evidence that the spellings in question were particularly associated either with Greene or with the printer of the work in question, namely John Wolfe.

which was used in a particular case would presumably depend mainly on the fancy of the compositor. To him they would be alternative spellings just as duety—duty, friend—frind—freind—frende, heard—hard, or man —manne, and equally unimportant. There is an exactly equal chance of his making variations in the first group as in the second, and the fact that 'percullis' or 'eughe' or 'mushrump' might seem to a modern student odd spellings worth taking notice of, and that 'manne' or 'freind' might not, is entirely beside the point.

Thus, suppose we find in three texts the following forms:

A	B	C
percullis	percullis	portcullis
thorough	through	through
sometimes	sometimes	sometime
trauail	trauail	trauel

we cannot take these as any evidence whatever of an A>B>C (or vice versa) relationship, unless we have satisfied ourselves that there are no variations such as

A	B	C
friend	freind	friend
hard	heard	hard
duety	duty	duety

which would suggest A>C>B or B>A>C relationship, but which, owing to their seeming less striking variations to *us*, we might easily overlook.

The only way, then, in which *selected* spellings, as distinguished from spellings considered *en masse*, can safely be taken as evidence of the relationship of texts is when we can definitely say that by the date of one or more of the texts under consideration these particular spellings had become antiquated, and that therefore a compositor was unlikely to use them if he had a later and current spelling in the text before him. Thus we might have in three dated editions the following:

A (1580)	B (1600)	C (1620)
sometimes	sometime	sometimes
percullis	portcullis	percullis

If we could satisfy ourselves that the spellings 'sometimes' (= formerly) and 'percullis' were going out of use by 1600, we could argue that in 1620 a compositor would be very unlikely to substitute these spellings if he had the normal 'sometime' and 'portcullis' before him, and that therefore edition C is more likely to have been printed from A than from B. As long, however, as two or more variant spellings are in common use the occurrence of one rather than the other in a particular text can, by itself, constitute no evidence whatever as to the edition from which it was printed.

TWO SPECIMEN PAGES FROM
THE OXFORD SHAKESPEARE
RICHARD III, I. iv. 267–II. i. 34

[The First Quarto of this play (1597), having been almost certainly printed from a 'report' and not from a transcript of the author's manuscript, affords no evidence as to the spelling or other details of that manuscript. The First Folio appears to have been printed from the Quarto of 1622 corrected in great part by an original manuscript of which some leaves had been lost and which had been completed by a transcript from an early Quarto, being thus for these portions ultimately dependent upon the First Quarto. The Folio text therefore, while no more likely to conform to the spelling of the author in *any* portion than the First Quarto, is likely to be much more correct as regards the greater part than that Quarto in respect of the wording. While a case could, I think, be made out either for using the First Quarto corrected by the Folio, or for using the Folio alone, as the basis of a reprint, the latter has been here preferred as giving a somewhat more uniform text. The question will be discussed in the separate introduction to the play.]

1. *Mur.* So do not I: go Coward as thou art.
  Well, Ile go hide the body in some hole,
  Till that the Duke giue order for his buriall:
  And when I haue my meede, I will away,   270
  For this will out, and then I must not stay.   *Exit.*

ACT II, Scene i.

Flourish.   [*1120*]

Enter the King sicke, the Queene [Elizabeth], Lord Marquesse
  Dorset, Riuers, Hastings, Catesby,
  Buckingham, Wooduill [, Scales].

K. Edw. Why so: now haue I done a good daies work.
  You Peeres, continue this vnited League:
  I, euery day expect an Embassage
  From my Redeemer, to redeeme me hence.
  And more in peace my soule shall part to heauen,   5
  Since I haue made my Friends at peace on earth.
  Hastings and *Riuers*, take each others hand,   [*1130*]

268 Well . . . the body] F1±: Now must
  I hide his body Qq, Camb.
269 Till that . . . giue] F1±: Vntill the
  Duke take Qq, Camb.
270 will] F1–Rowe, Cap., Mal., Tho.:
  must Qq, Pope–Johns., Camb.
271 then] F1±: here Qq, Camb.
II. i.] *New act* F1+ (*Actus Secundus.*
  Scœna Prima. F1): *not divided* Qq
  Scene: *London. The palace.* Camb.
  s.d. *Enter King, Queene, Hastings,*
  Ryuers, Dorcet, &c. Qq (*om. Dorcet,*
  Q3–6)

Catesby, *om.* Cap.+
Wooduill] *Grey* Cap.+
Scales] Ed.
1 Why . . . haue I] F1+: So, now I haue
  Qq
5 more in] Rowe, Ste. '93: now in Qq,
  Pope–Johns., Mal.+: more to Ff:
  more at Cap.
to] from Q1, 2. *See note*
6 made] F1±: set Qq, Camb.
7 *Hastings* and *Riuers*] Rowe–Johns.:
  Riuers and Hastings Qq, Cap.+:
  Dorset and Riuers Ff

II. i. Edward's attempt to reconcile the opposing factions just before his death
is recorded by More, who specifically mentions the grievances of the Queen,
Dorset, and Rivers against Hastings (Holinshed, ed. 1807–8, iii. 363; Halle, ed.
1809, 343–4). That Edward revoked the order for Clarence's death seems to have
no basis in historical fact, though More's narrative (Hol. 362, Halle 342) and the
chroniclers' earlier account of his death refer to the King's repentance—the latter
in a passage which undoubtedly inspired the fictitious incident of Derby's boon;
'But sure it is, that although king Edward were consenting to his death; yet he
much did both lament his infortunate chance, & repent his sudden execution:
insomuch that when anie person sued to him for the pardon of malefactors con-
demned to death, he would accustomablie saie, & openlie speake: "Oh infortunate
brother, for whose life not one would make sute"' (Hol. 346, Halle 326).

  5 *to.* Steevens, in his reprint, gave 'for' from an unspecified source. This was
adopted by Grant White.

Dissemble not your hatred, Sweare your loue.

Riu. By heauen, my soule is purg'd from grudging hate
And with my hand I seale my true hearts Loue.   10

Hast. So thriue I, as I truly sweare the like.

K. Edw. Take heed you dally not before your King,
Lest he that is the supreme King of Kings
Confound your hidden falshood, and award
Either of you to be the others end.   15

Hast. So prosper I, as I sweare perfect loue.

Riu. And I, as I loue *Hastings* with my heart.   [*1140*]

K. Edw. Madam, your selfe is not exempt from this:
Nor you Sonne *Dorset*, *Buckingham* nor you;
You haue bene factious one against the other.   20
Wife, loue Lord *Hastings*, let him kisse your hand,
And what you do, do it vnfeignedly.

Q. Eliz. There *Hastings*, I will neuer more remember
Our former hatred, so thriue I, and mine.

K. Edw. *Dorset*, imbrace him: *Hastings*, loue Lord Marquesse.   25

Dor. This interchange of loue, I heere protest   [*1150*]
Vpon my part, shall be inuiolable.

Hast. And so sweare I.

K. Edw. Now Princely *Buckingham*, seale yᵘ this league
With thy embracements to my wiues Allies,   30
And make me happy in your vnity.

Buck. When euer *Buckingham* doth turne his hate
Vpon your Grace, but with all dutious loue,
Doth cherish you, and yours, God punish me

9 soule] F1＋: heart Qq
18 is] F1–Johns., Tho.: are Qq, Cap.–
Camb.
from] F1–Johns., Tho.: in Qq, Cap.–
Camb.
19 you Sonne] F1–Rowe, Tho.: your
son Qq, Pope–Camb. *See note*
23 There] F1 ±: Here Qq, Camb.
25 *One line* Rowe iii＋: *two ll.* (...him:/

Hastings...) F1–Rowe ii: *om.* Qq
26–7 protestₐ . . . part,] F1–Rowe ii,
Tho.: protest, . . . partₐ Qq, Camb.:
protest, . . . part, Rowe iii–Mal.
27 inuiolable] F1 ±: vnuiolable Qq,
Camb.
28 I] F1 ±: I my Lord Qq, Camb.
32–3 s.D. *To the Queen.* Rowe＋
33 Vpon your Grace] F1 ±: On you or

19 *you Sonne Dorset*. This was Thomas Grey, born 1451, elder son of Sir Thomas
Grey whose widow married Edward IV, and was therefore the Queen's son and the
King's step-son. Either 'you son Dorset' or 'your son Dorset' would have been
historically correct.

30 *wiues*, i.e. wife's.   *Allies*, i.e. kindred.

33–4 *but* . . . *Doth cherish*, i.e. and does not cherish.